A **UDL** NOW!

Universal Design for Learning in MATHEMATICS Instruction K-5

KATIE NOVAK and ASHLEY MARLOW

CAST | Until learning has no limits.

© 2025 CAST, Inc.

All rights reserved. No part of this publication may be reproduced, stored in a retrieval system, or transmitted in any form or by any means, electronic, mechanical, photocopying, recording, or otherwise, without the prior permission of the Publisher.

ISBN (paperback) 978-1-943085-30-9
ISBN (ebook) 978-1-943085-31-6
Library of Congress Control Number 2024946210
Cover Design: Lindie Johnson
Interior Design and Cover Production: Happenstance Type-O-Rama

Published by CAST Professional Publishing, an imprint of CAST, Inc., Lynnfield, Massachusetts, USA

For information about special discounts for bulk purchases, please email publishing@cast.org or visit https://publishing.cast.org.

To Torin, Aylin, Brec, Boden, Jack, and Charlie. May you always embrace your inner math person.

Love, your moms

Contents

Introduction: Sparking Inclusive Practices in Mathematics 1

1 Math Education: Where It Has Been and Where It Needs to Go 7

2 Breaking the Echo: Mathematics as Inquiry and Inclusion 23

3 Growing Positive Mathematical Mindsets for Teachers and Students 39

4 Cultivating Early Numeracy Skills 55

5 Unlock Access to Additive Reasoning 67

6 Deepening Multiplication and Division Understanding 87

7 Inviting Students Into the World of Fractions 97

Conclusion 111

References 117
Index 121
About the Authors 129

Introduction

Sparking Inclusive Practices in Mathematics

There is a classic scene in the Alfred Hitchcock movie *To Catch a Thief* where the characters played by Cary Grant and Grace Kelly smooch on a terrace overlooking the French Riviera against a background of fireworks. This scene represents "sparks flying" between the two characters. The metaphor of "sparks flying" doesn't always have to be romantic, though. Sometimes, it denotes the physical generation of sparks, implying a forceful collision charged with energy. This interpretation beautifully captures our first meeting, when Ashley's expertise in equitable, inclusive mathematics instruction collided with Katie's in Universal Design for Learning (UDL).

No, we didn't meet on a terrace overlooking the French Riviera, although that would have been amazing! We met at a conference held at the Killington Grand Resort Hotel in Vermont that focused on building more inclusive systems with the Vermont Superintendents Association. Teams from around the state assembled to create strategic plans to be more inclusive and ensure that students, especially those with the most significant support needs, had access to grade-level classrooms with their peers, as mandated by Act 173—a law enacted by the State of Vermont in 2018 to enhance the effectiveness, availability, and equity of services

Universal Design for Learning in Mathematics Instruction (K–5)

provided to all students who require additional support in Vermont's schools.

Act 173 is a significant piece of legislation that fundamentally changed how special education is funded and how general education and intervention services are delivered to students with significant support needs to ensure they have equitable access to inclusive and rigorous learning environments with their peers in all content areas. The act is intended to support students with an individualized education program (IEP), students with a 504 plan under the Rehabilitation Act of 1973, and students who have neither an IEP nor a 504 but whose ability to learn is hampered by a disability or by social, emotional, or behavioral needs. Act 173 is also intended to support all students who are English learners and students who read below grade level (Vermont Agency of Education, 2024).

Inclusion is critical in all grades and subjects, and we firmly believe that all students should have access to instruction in classrooms alongside their peers. That being said, some content areas have become more inclusive than others, and one of the areas that creates the biggest hurdles to access and inclusion is—you guessed it—mathematics.

The lack of access to rigorous mathematics education and the importance of removing barriers to that access have been documented for decades. The Algebra Project, founded by civil rights activist and mathematician Robert Moses, provides a case study that highlights the importance of ensuring that all students, especially those historically resilient and institutionally marginalized in math education, gain access early on to critical mathematical concepts. His idea was revolutionary at the time: to treat math as a civil right. Yet, decades later, many students still do not have access to rigorous mathematics instruction. According to the 2022 results from the National Assessment of Educational Progress (NAEP), also known as the Nation's Report Card, the average mathematics scores for fourth and eighth graders have significantly declined.

Introduction

The 2022 report highlights that average math scores for fourth graders fell by five points and for eighth graders by eight points compared to 2019, marking the largest decline in mathematics since the assessment began in 1990. Only 36% of fourth graders who completed the assessment and 26% of all eighth graders who completed the assessment were rated at or above the proficient level in mathematics, indicating a lack of proficiency in fundamental mathematical skills necessary for higher-level problem-solving and reasoning (Nation's Report Card, 2022).

The most devastating findings underscore the growing disparities in achievement between high-performing and low-performing students, suggesting that the most vulnerable populations are the hardest hit. We cannot ignore the devastating reality that many students, particularly those who are historically resilient and institutionally marginalized, continue to face inequitable access to quality mathematics education. We also want you to remember that these statistics do not define our students' potential. Rather, they underscore the urgent need for change.

Over lunch from the Make-Your-Own-Taco Bar (a delightful nod to the principles of UDL!) at the Killington Grand Resort Hotel, we discussed our current realities, like the results found in the Nation's Report Card, and our collective passion for working to dismantle the systems that continue to perpetuate these outcomes. Following that conference, we decided to write an article together. We pitched an article to Edutopia, "Making Math Accessible for All Students," and were thrilled when it was published. In the article, we wrote:

> All students can build mastery in mathematics when the conditions are right. Access to excellent math instruction for all students creates opportunities for higher learning and ultimately better lives. For students to be successful in learning math, they must demonstrate reasoning and sense-making of math concepts.
>
> Specifically, all students need to demonstrate success in algebra to open pathways into college and careers. If algebra is the

gatekeeper to future success, we can open this gate by teaching mathematics through the lens of Universal Design for Learning (UDL). UDL is a framework that provides students with opportunities to work toward firm goals through flexible means.

When used in mathematics classrooms, UDL helps minimize barriers that prevent students from seeing themselves as capable problem-solvers with agency as mathematicians. For students to reach their full potential as "math people," all learners must participate in meaningful, challenging learning opportunities. (Marlow & Novak, 2022)

As soon as the article was released, our amazing editors, David Gordon and Billie Fitzpatrick, reached out and said, "We loved the article. You two need to write a book together." And so, here it is.

This book is for K–5 mathematics teachers to learn more about how to support all students to learn at high levels in mathematics. While we acknowledge the sobering statistics on math proficiency in the United States, it's important to recognize that this book is not centered on those figures. We hope to provide a resource for teachers to reflect on their current practice and learning experience in math and ask themselves: *What can I do to improve the math learning experience for me and my students? How do I create a math learning environment that sends the message that we are all capable mathematicians? What support and additional professional learning would I benefit from to make this happen?*

In this text, we combine our knowledge in both UDL and mathematics education to build on the critical work of the Algebra Project and the importance of rigorous mathematics as a civil right. As members of the UDL community—a steadily growing, tight-knit network—we feel incredibly humbled to publish CAST's first book about UDL focused solely on mathematics. We are driven by a shared belief that a decline in math achievement is unacceptable, especially given the hard work of educators and the clear evidence of what works in mathematics education. As you explore these pages, we invite you to ignite your inner inclusive practice gladiator and discover the "math person" within each of your students, thereby reshaping your educational landscape to best meet the needs of all learners. Let the sparks fly—marking the beginning of a journey toward equitable education for every student.

Reflection Question

1. As you embark on reading this book, what specific goals do you have in mind to enhance your teaching practice, especially in making math accessible to all students? Consider sharing your goals with a colleague or on social media to create a dialogue around overcoming educational barriers and fostering inclusivity through UDL.

"mimic" the procedure (Liljedahl, 2020). Often, this practice was completed through rote repetition and required to be completed independently. Further, teachers demanded that regular practice included a timed component. Does memorizing and reciting your times tables ring a bell?

This approach to teaching math signaled to students that there was one way to "do math." Even today in traditional math classrooms, we often see an "I do, we do, you do" approach to scaffolding the lesson. For example, the teacher states, "This is how you solve a subtraction problem with regrouping." The teacher models one strategy, often without a visual or concrete model, and then asks the class to replicate that same strategy as a group. The class solves another sample problem together, one or two answers are written on a whiteboard, and the teacher scans the room for correct and incorrect answers. Once the teacher sees enough correct answers, the class returns to their desks to practice independently, often repeating the same procedure the teacher prescribed. Students who don't understand the procedure are often perceived as incapable of doing math. In this learning environment, students are excluded from the opportunity to think, be challenged, compare their thinking with others, and make sense of mathematics. They spend most of their math learning time regurgitating a procedure they've memorized (with or without true understanding) or not engaging at all—both scenarios in which the student is not actively thinking about and doing mathematics (Liljedahl, 2020).

In such a learning environment, students are often segregated into homogenous groupings based on their perceived abilities, further emphasizing the divide between the knowers and doers of math and their apparent opposites. This division reflects the persistent implementation of *tracking*, or the separation of students based on academic ability for instruction into different academic paths, starting as early as elementary school (McCardle, 2020).

Math pedagogy emphasizing "do it like me" with rote repetition also sends the message that the teacher is the keeper of the knowledge. They are the doers and thinkers of mathematics, and the students are trying to keep up. Students who are not able to memorize the steps in a given procedure fall further and further behind their peers who can regurgitate those steps and compute accurately. We often hear from teachers who can readily recall a procedure like "keep, change, flip" to divide a fraction by another fraction. However, when we ask teachers to generate a word problem that involves dividing fractions or identify a situation in their real lives when they might need this computation, it can be a challenge. Thus, students who can easily memorize and mimic a procedure are perceived as strong mathematicians, while others who may understand through visual modeling or context creation—both much more complex and higher-order forms of thinking than memorization—are perceived as less competent in mathematics.

Stand and deliver math instruction with rote practice has perpetuated a system where many students choose to avoid higher levels of mathematics. Unfortunately, this excludes them from college and career opportunities in the STEM field that might be of interest to them. Teachers invested in disrupting this system have to do the difficult work of dismantling their own unhelpful beliefs about the learning and teaching of mathematics, unlearning those teaching practices, and relearning more inclusive pedagogy. Simultaneously, they are rebuilding their own math content knowledge of the grade bands they teach. A history of math education that prioritizes a single approach for solving math problems, focusing on the teacher's strategy, has led to an unjust and inequitable system for our students and teachers. In chapters 2 and 3, we will further explore the impact on teacher training and negative mindsets toward math for both teachers and students.

The Access and Equity Issue

According to the 2017–18 National Teacher and Principal Survey (NTPS), 79% of public school teachers identified as White and non-Hispanic; 9% as Hispanic; 7% as Black and non-Hispanic; 2% as Asian and non-Hispanic; 2% as two or more races and non-Hispanic; and less than 1% as either Native Hawaiian/Pacific Islander, non-Hispanic, or American Indian/Alaska Native, non-Hispanic. All this to say, the majority of educators in the United States identify as White (NTPS, 2017–18). Yet less than half of students in grades K–12 in the United States identify as White (Fabina et al., 2023). When we consider race, sexual orientation, gender, and other statistics related to historically resilient and institutionally underserved populations, there is a vast discrepancy between teachers' identities (both visible and invisible) and those of their students.

Why does this matter? Consider the "do it like me" approach to math teaching and learning. A pattern of emphasis on rote memorization and surface-level recall, delivered by teachers who often do not share the same identities as their students, sends the message that the teacher's strategy and visible identity reflect the people who can do the math. Intentionally or unintentionally, this has led to a system of tracking that includes gifted and talented math education programs with predictable memberships based on demographics. Disproportionate access to academic tracks that lead to high levels of math learning in turn leads to disproportionate access to college and career opportunities for our institutionally underserved populations. When procedural pedagogy and tracking practices are in place, we limit the opportunities for many students, especially our students of color and students with IEPs.

Addressing Inequities With UDL

Unfortunately, historically resilient and institutionally underserved student groups have often been deprived of equitable access to high-quality, affirming, and humanizing math instruction. This disparity is a consequence of the deep-rooted systemic barriers entrenched in our educational system (Goffney et al., 2018). Universal Design for Learning (UDL) provides a framework for dismantling the inequitable teaching practices embedded in "do it like me" and tracking systems in math education. At the heart of UDL lies a powerful call to recognize and honor the humanity of our students when designing their learning experiences. UDL challenges us to dismantle these barriers and harness our power and privilege to co-create learning experiences with our students, giving them a voice and choice (Chardin & Novak, 2020).

The goal of UDL is to support learning that is purposeful and reflective; resourceful and authentic; and strategic and action-oriented. The UDL framework embraces diversity at its core—our students show up as their authentic, unique selves, and our responsibility as educators is to design instruction so that all learners have equitable access. UDL also reminds us there is no such thing as an average student. In contrast, a learning environment centered on procedure and "do it like me" pedagogy does not recognize variability. With UDL, teachers remove barriers to learning by considering, celebrating, and designing for variability in any learning environment. UDL embraces the variability of our learners and challenges teachers to hold rigorous expectations for *all* students while providing ramps for *all* of them to get there.

Inclusive teaching practices in math align with this framework while providing specific action steps we can take in our classrooms to create a learning environment that provides meaningful access to grade-level learning for all students. These inclusive practices include an emphasis on math dialogue, where the thinking is held among the students rather than the teacher. The teacher is the facilitator, supporting students in making connections between models, strategies, and key mathematical concepts. Inclusive math instruction supports justification and reasoning as part of sense-making, emphasizing conceptual understanding over rote memorization. Such an approach nurtures an environment where diverse mathematical ideas are valued, and students are encouraged to articulate their problem-solving processes while comparing their thinking with others.

Students learn to communicate effectively through regular conversations about the math they do. Humanizing mathematics ensures that *all* students' voices are heard, and diverse ideas are valued in the classroom community (Tan et al., 2020). We expect all students to engage in meaningful conversations about mathematics. In that case, we must create a learning environment that promotes opportunities to ask questions, share thinking, and compare thinking with others.

While lack of access to grade-level learning opportunities in math education contributes significantly to the achievement gap, a structured approach to implementing UDL can address these disparities. UDL ensures that all students have equitable access to challenging grade-level mathematics content. It's about not only providing resources but also utilizing them effectively to promote inclusive, high-quality learning experiences for every student, laying a foundation for successful outcomes in mathematics. UDL principles play a key role in this process by offering three core elements: multiple means of engagement, representation, and action and expression.

Multiple Means of Engagement

Engaging a student is a little like plugging in a lamp. It doesn't matter what shade we buy or what lightbulb we use: If there is no electricity, there is no light. If there is no engagement, there is no learning. In math instruction, engagement goes beyond merely sparking interest or "turning on the light"; it involves creating a learning environment where students are clear on the purpose of each lesson, have options and choices to access the lesson, actively participate in mathematical discourse, make connections between ideas, and collectively expand their knowledge through reflection and sense-making opportunities.

Understanding the goal of each math lesson, aligned to grade-level learning, is crucial. This clarity not only aligns with the broader objectives of UDL but also ensures that students grasp the purpose behind their learning activities. When students comprehend what they're aiming to achieve in each lesson, it boosts their motivation and engagement. This understanding aids them in connecting the dots between various mathematical concepts, enhancing their overall learning experience. Our task as educators is to articulate these goals clearly, helping students see the relevance and application of their learning in a broader context. By being clear about our goals, we recruit interest and help students sustain effort and persistence when things get challenging. Being clear about the purpose of each lesson and communicating that to students also helps them make more responsible decisions about their learning when we provide them with options and choices.

Choice is often referred to as a hallmark of UDL, but how choice is offered is often misunderstood. The aim is not simply to offer choices but to ensure all students have pathways that enable access to grade-level instruction. The UDL Guidelines 3.0 emphasize shifting away from practices that may seem too prescriptive or teacher-centric—where educators provide choices—to approaches that empower students to navigate, engage, and construct their learning experiences. The UDL Guidelines are not designed to be a tool for educators to implement but rather a framework for learners to use in shaping their own educational journeys. Students may need to choose different resources, strategies, and/or materials to make meaning, and so teachers need to shift the opportunities they provide for students to understand new concepts and demonstrate this thinking and reasoning. One helpful consideration in UDL is "firm goals, flexible means." When students have options to access scaffolds, supports, or additional challenges, all pathways must lead students toward and beyond the mastery of grade-level standards.

Sometimes educators also consider UDL a "fun meter." A better way to think about UDL is a "worthwhile meter." Students need options and choices to know that learning is possible and worthwhile and that if they continue to persist, they will have the support they need to experience success. To foster collaboration and collective learning, we must ensure students have ongoing opportunities to reflect on their learning journey. This reflection encourages self-awareness and helps them identify their learning strengths and needs. Teachers need to enable students to make choices, support their self-awareness, and build a trusting relationship that emphasizes, "I see you, I believe in you, and it's my responsibility to provide options that meet your needs and interests."

Equally important is addressing social-emotional factors to maintain a positive learning environment. Establishing clear classroom norms and expectations, promoting active listening, and creating an atmosphere where mistakes are celebrated as learning opportunities as students work toward grade-level standards can build trust and a sense of belonging among students.

Multiple Means of Representation

In math instruction, the UDL principle of multiple means of representation broadens our understanding of how students comprehend and engage with mathematical concepts. It emphasizes the significance of presenting information in diverse ways to cater to the variability of learners as they build comprehension.

To effectively implement multiple means of representation, math educators can ensure that students know how to access various tools, materials, and techniques. Students need opportunities to build their understanding of math through concrete manipulatives and visual representations, which then enable them to apply that understanding to abstract concepts (Tapper, 2012). Concrete models like base ten blocks, tens frames, number lines, and fraction bars allow students to manipulate math physically. Visual models and representations, such as area models, graphs, charts, and diagrams, can help students grasp abstract concepts and see the relationships between different elements. For example, when teaching functions, visually representing the function as a table can aid students in understanding how inputs and outputs relate to each other. When developing multiplicative reasoning, we can help a student build their understanding of unitizing by showing a group of 3 objects as a single unit that can be skip-counted 4 times to make a total of 12 objects (see Figure 1.1).

Similarly, providing auditory representations, such as verbal explanations or audio recordings, benefits students who learn best through listening and oral processing. A teacher may use verbal instructions to guide students through a complex problem-solving process or provide audio descriptions of geometric shapes to enhance spatial reasoning.

Technology is another valuable resource for providing multiple means of representation. Interactive simulations and educational software can offer dynamic visualizations, interactive

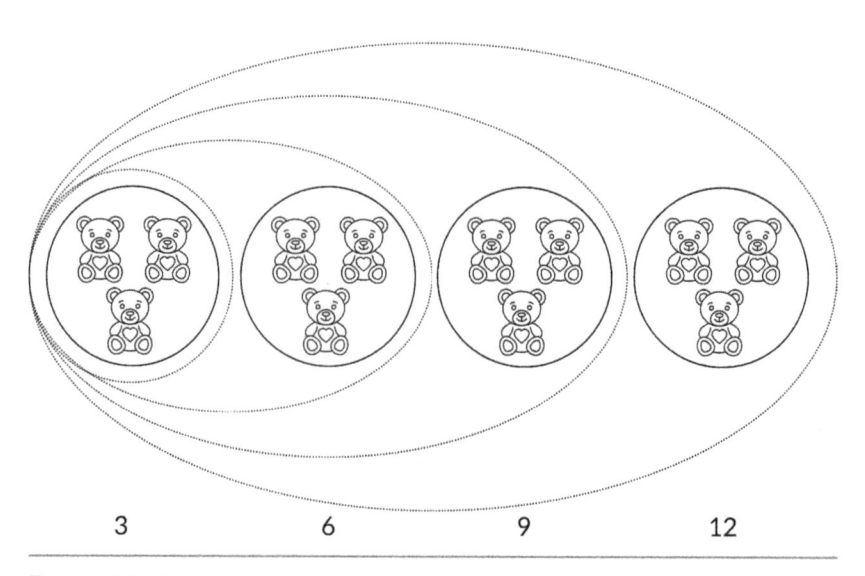

Figure 1.1. Visual models can help students grasp abstract concepts.

activities, and virtual manipulatives, enabling students to explore mathematical concepts in a personalized and engaging manner. As students gain proficiency in interpreting and expressing mathematical ideas through various modes, they become more flexible and adaptable problem solvers, equipped to tackle diverse mathematical challenges with creativity and ingenuity.

Multiple Means of Action and Expression

The UDL principle of multiple means of action and expression recognizes students' diverse strengths, needs, and preferences when demonstrating their understanding of and communicating mathematical ideas. It highlights the importance of providing a wide range of opportunities for students to showcase their knowledge and skills through various means while also taking into account their executive function support needs.

Math educators can effectively implement multiple means of action and expression by encouraging students to demonstrate their understanding using different modes and formats. While written assessments are common, they do not capture the full capabilities of all learners. Allowing students to choose from various options for presenting their work can better accommodate their individual variability. For instance, some students may excel at articulating their ideas through written explanations, while others may prefer to create visual representations or conduct a one-on-one student interview to demonstrate their understanding.

Additionally, incorporating technology into math assignments can expand students' choices for expressing their mathematical ideas. In Ashley's third-grade classroom, students used a voice recording tool to take a picture of their work and describe their mathematical thinking. Educational software, multimedia presentations, and online platforms offer innovative ways for students to showcase their knowledge. With these tools, students can express their thinking and comments through drawing, in writing, or by recording their voice to connect and compare their ideas with those of their peers. Students can use interactive graphs or design simulations to illustrate complex mathematical concepts, demonstrating their proficiency through engaging and interactive projects.

Offering a range of tools, strategies, and accommodations can empower students to work toward grade-level math standards, even if they face executive function challenges. Ensuring that students have clear and structured task instructions, visual cues, and checklists can help them systematically organize their thoughts and approach assignments. Breaking down complex math problems into smaller, manageable steps can also assist students with executive function difficulties in tackling challenges more effectively. It is likewise beneficial to incorporate executive function skill-building activities—such as time management exercises, goal-setting discussions, and self-monitoring reflections—into math lessons. Removing the expectation of memorization and speed is important when we want all students to learn math well.

Fostering a more inclusive and supportive learning environment by offering flexible assignment formats and allowing students to choose options that suit their strengths and needs equips all students to thrive and succeed in demonstrating their mathematical proficiency. This approach empowers students and enhances their overall engagement and enjoyment in learning.

In essence, UDL challenges us to be conscious and compassionate architects of education, designing learning experiences that transcend rigid norms and uplift the humanity of every student. By creating an environment where all students are seen, heard, and valued, we cultivate within each learner a deep love for math as well as confidence, competence, and purpose.

Using the UDL framework to design learning experiences in math supports this type of environment. UDL is inherently inclusive and embraces the idea that everyone has something of value to contribute in math class. The goal is to create a space where students feel comfortable sharing ideas, making mistakes, sitting in this discomfort confidently, and productively struggling to make sense of mathematical concepts. This is true inclusion—when everyone feels they belong and adds value to the classroom learning environment. Table 1-1 shares reflection questions that may help you as you reflect on your current learning environment in math.

Table 1-1: UDL Considerations in Math

Provide Multiple Means of Engagement	Provide Multiple Means of Representation	Provide Multiple Means of Action and Expression
★ How do you ensure all students participate in a welcoming, inclusive number sense routine? ★ What strategies are in place for students to share their ideas with peers? ★ How do you structure groups to help students practice priority concepts, especially if they have unfinished learning?	★ How do you utilize learning targets visually and verbally to confirm that students understand the learning goal? ★ In what ways do you facilitate meaning-making through multiple models and representations? ★ Where is there evidence of mathematical thinking visible around the learning space?	★ Where are the math manipulatives or tools located? Are they easily accessible for students to use independently? ★ How do you use the choice of activities to encourage students to take ownership of their learning and express their thinking in their own way?

A "Do It Like Me" Example Redefined

Incorporating UDL into mathematics instruction involves transforming conventional "do it like me" teaching practices into more inclusive, engaging, and effective methods. Let's consider how we might reimagine a traditional math task to overcome barriers and embrace the diversity of learners.

Universal Design for Learning in Mathematics Instruction (K–5)

Teacher: "Solve 10 − 3 = ___ on your board. When time is up, we will all show our answers, and I'll let you know who is correct."

Students: Work quietly on their boards. They reveal their work when the timer goes off. The teacher looks at the answers and says yes or no to each student to indicate whether they are correct.

Teacher: "Great job! You start at 10 and count back 3 like this: 9, 8, 7. So, the answer is 7. Let's do another one, and then you will practice more problems like this in your notebook."

There are a few barriers to accessing the math lesson in this situation. First, timing creates a barrier for several students to get started, leading to anxiety and diverting their brainpower to worrying instead of thinking. Second, students work in isolation rather than collaboratively, so those who aren't sure how to start end up sitting there, stuck. Third, the implication that there is only one way to solve the problem prevents some students from conceptualizing it in a way that makes sense to them. In this scenario, the teacher prioritizes a "do it like me" approach, focusing on explaining and practicing a single targeted strategy.

Consider this UDL-inspired redesign of the math lesson that supports inclusion and access for all students:

Teacher: *Shows an image of 10 apples organized in 2 rows of 5, similar to a tens frame.* "What do you notice? What are you wondering about these apples?"

Students: "I notice there are 10 apples! I notice they are all red. I wonder how we could share them?"

Teacher: "Wow! Those are really interesting wonders. I was wondering what would happen if these 10 apples were on my counter at home and each of my kids took one to school. I have three kids. How many would I have left?" *The students raise their hands to share.*

Teacher: *"I am going to put you in random groups of three, and I want you to show me all of the ways we could solve this problem. Sit wherever you'd like in the room together, and remember, there are lots of math tools on the shelf by the carpet that you can use to help show your thinking!"*

The shelf includes whiteboards, dry-erase markers, paper, pencils, and bins of items to count, like tiny plastic bears and Unifix Cubes.

The students sit around the room, working collaboratively to show all of the ways they could solve the problem. The teacher walks around the room, checking in on student understanding, asking clarifying questions, sorting the strategies, and sequencing their complexity in their notes to prepare for students to share.

Teacher: *"It was so interesting seeing all the different ways you could solve this problem. Let's share some of the strategies!"*

The teacher then intentionally calls groups up to share one of their models and strategies, moving from concrete to more abstract. The goal is for all students to see their own thinking represented and have the opportunity to consider another way. Some student strategies include:

- "We started at 10 apples and took away 2 and then 1 more because 2 plus 1 equals 3, and we had to take away 3, so now you can see there are 5 and 2 more left, and that's 7."
- "We know that 7 and 3 make 10, so we knew right away that eating 3 would leave us with 7."
- "We used a bead string with 10 beads and started at the 5 and then counted up 2 more. Oh, that was after we slid over the 3 taken to school."

After reflecting on the lesson transformation, consider how the teacher's role in universally designed classrooms shifts from being the sole disseminator of information to a facilitator of learning, guiding students through exploration and discovery.

As we have shared throughout this chapter, the "do it like me" approach in mathematics instruction stifles creativity and ignores students' diverse cognitive and cultural backgrounds. This book asks you to sit in that discomfort and consider alternative teaching practices that are more inclusive and engaging for all of your students. The hard work of unlearning, relearning, and then designing proactively for the variability of your students is worth it. Your current and future students will thank you and may come back to say, "I love math now," too.

REFLECTION QUESTIONS

1. Reflect on the historical "I do, we do, you do" model of math instruction compared to the UDL framework discussed. How do these approaches differ in their assumptions about student capabilities and roles in the learning process?

2. Reflect on your own teaching practice in relation to the traditional "I do, we do, you do" model and the UDL framework discussed in the chapter. How could shifting to a UDL framework impact your approach to teaching mathematics?

3. The chapter highlights the three core principles of UDL: multiple means of engagement, multiple means of representation, and multiple means of action and expression. Discuss specific strategies and examples for incorporating these principles into math instruction to create a more inclusive and engaging learning environment.

4. Imagine the long-term effects on your students if you implemented UDL in your math classes. How might this shift affect their academic outcomes, self-perception as learners, and future opportunities?

2

Breaking the Echo

Mathematics as Inquiry and Inclusion

The Curse of Echo

In a tragic Greek myth, the wood nymph Echo enrages Hera, the queen of the gods, who retaliates by cursing Echo with the inability to communicate other than to repeat what has just been said to her. Research shows that many K–12 students have a similar curse when it comes to mathematics instruction. As we shared in the previous chapter, instead of thinking creatively and working collaboratively to solve problems, students are often taught the "do it like me" approach, where they are expected to repeat what they have learned, copy math facts on worksheets or problems off the board, and echo explanations shared in one-size-fits-all direct instruction.

Just as Echo was cursed to repeat others' words, many students are trapped in a system that prioritizes mimicking the teacher's strategy or solving a problem one way, perpetuating the belief that some learners can do math and some can't.

Transforming math instruction involves developing and including math tasks that provide opportunities for students to justify or argue their thinking, compare their thinking with others, and model their strategies through visual, concrete, and abstract representations. Such an approach nurtures an environment where diverse mathematical ideas are valued, and students are encouraged to think deeply about the concepts. This shift from passive to active learning is essential in breaking the curse of Echo in mathematics education.

The Illusion of Quality in Quantity

School districts are channeling millions of dollars annually into securing high-quality instructional materials. Providing materials alone proves insufficient. An investigation conducted by Equity Trust (Dysarz, 2018), which scrutinized over 1,800 middle-level mathematics assignments, discovered a concerning trend. While 70% of these assignments aligned with grade-level standards, less than one-third of the assignments prompted students to communicate their thinking or justify their responses. Most baffling? Only 9% of the assignments pushed student thinking to higher levels. Yet the Common Core State Standards for Mathematical Practice, a supplement to the Common Core State Standards for Mathematical Content, emphasize the importance of developing student mathematicians who can make sense of problems and persevere in solving them, construct viable arguments and critique others' reasoning, model with mathematics, and look for and make use of structure and repeated reasoning—all evidence of thinking mathematically at higher levels (National Governors Association Center for Best Practices, Council of Chief State School Officers, 2010).

After acknowledging the pitfalls of the "do it like me" approach and the pressing need for a shift in teaching methods, we must confront the paradox highlighted by the Equity Trust

In her influential book *Culturally Responsive Teaching and the Brain*, Zaretta Hammond (2014) emphasizes that all students can handle the cognitive load of challenging tasks when teachers connect learning to students' cultural contexts. Hammond's approach is not just about making connections for the sake of relevance; it's about challenging students with rigorous tasks that are meaningful and engaging. This method makes math more accessible and relevant, encouraging students to actively engage with challenging content.

Teachers can help students engage with mathematics by using these contexts to make mathematical content meaningful. Students are more likely to engage in mathematics when asked to solve problems that are relevant, realistic, worthwhile, enjoyable, and motivating. When students see the math they do as authentic, purposeful, and related to their lived experiences, they are more likely to engage in sense-making and higher-order thinking. As a third-grade teacher, Ashley encountered a math problem stating that a person had 93 sheets of paper on their desk and another 57 in their backpack and asking students to solve for the total number. She tried to start the problem by encouraging students to visualize the situation. A student raised their hand and said, "Um . . . Mrs. Marlow, why does she have so much paper, and why is she counting every sheet?" The whole class started to laugh because, truly, why *did* this person know they had exactly 93 sheets of paper? What's the story here?

Integrating real-life scenarios into mathematics education is pivotal for fostering a genuine connection between students and the subject matter. By presenting math in contexts that mirror the students' experiences, we enhance engagement and deepen their understanding. The tasks that follow model this approach. They are not just math exercises; they are stories in which students can see themselves, making math accessible and relevant. This real-world relevance helps demystify mathematics, transforming it from abstract numbers and equations into a tool for navigating and making sense of the world around them.

Kindergarten Sample Task

Math Concept	Sample Task
Count to tell the number of objects within 10.	Mr. Garcia's class is having a bake sale to earn money toward their field trip. Lucia brought some cupcakes. Camila brought some more cupcakes. What do you notice? What do you wonder? How many cupcakes do they have all together?

Grades 1 and 2 Sample Task

Math Concept	Sample Task
Fluently add and subtract within 100 using strategies based on place value, properties of operations, and/or the relationship between addition and subtraction.	Ms. Shelby's class is sharing collections from home to practice counting large collections of items. Jackson and Marissa love to collect soccer cards, so they both brought in cards to share with the class. Jackson counted 48 cards in his collection, and Marissa counted 63 cards in her collection. ★ What do you notice about their collections? ★ What's the difference between Jackson's collection and Marissa's collection? How do you know?

Grades 3 and 4 Sample Task

Math Concept	Sample Task
Multiply whole numbers using strategies based on place value and the properties of operations.	Camden buys a slushie every Friday after school. A slushie drink at the corner store costs $1.98, including tax. About how many weeks can Camden buy a slushie with the $20 he earned from mowing a neighbor's lawn?

Grade 5 Sample Task

Math Concept	Sample Task
Solve word problems involving addition and subtraction of fractions referring to the same whole.	Jerome is making s'mores treats with his friend Martin. He has some leftover chocolate in the cupboard to use. He has about ⅓ of a chocolate bar from one package and ¾ of a chocolate bar from another package. He hopes to have enough for a full chocolate bar. Do you think he has enough?

Consider polling your students to generate ideas for relevant contexts a few times a year. Questions may include: *What do you like to do on the weekends? What is your favorite show, movie, or book? What is your favorite animal? What sports teams do you support?* Connecting with your students about their interests sends the message that they matter and that you see them and want to proactively design a learning environment that feels relevant to their lived experiences. Beyond changing names and numbers, you can tweak the actual context of tasks in your core programs to increase relevance for your students.

Supporting Access to High-Cognitive-Demand Math Tasks

Cognitive demand refers to the forms of thinking required to complete a mathematics task. As students develop their mathematical reasoning, they need access to tasks that allow them to think and build their understanding. Tasks that are low in cognitive demand require recalling facts or definitions or applying procedures. Tasks with high cognitive demand require students to use reasoning and make connections (Stein et al., 2000). This relates to Webb's Depth of Knowledge (DOK), a framework designed by Norman Webb of the University of Wisconsin Center for Educational Research to categorize tasks according to the complexity of thinking required to successfully complete them. The framework is divided into four levels:

> **DOK Level 1: Recall and Reproduction** This level involves basic recall of facts, definitions, or simple procedures. Tasks require a straightforward process and have a clear, correct answer. An example of a math task at DOK Level 1 might be, "If Cameron has 8 apples and wants 4 apples in each basket, how many apples will each basket contain?" At this level, students are simply applying a direct division operation without any higher-order thinking or reasoning.

DOK Level 2: Skills and Concepts At this level, students engage in some mental processing beyond recalling or reproducing a response. This might include comparing, organizing, summarizing, predicting, estimating, or interpreting data. Tasks at this level often require students to make some decisions about how to approach the problem. Consider how this math task builds on Level 1: "Cameron has 8 apples. Show all the ways Cameron could organize those apples into baskets, ensuring the same number of apples are in each basket." This question requires some conceptual understanding and basic reasoning.

DOK Level 3: Strategic Thinking Level 3 requires reasoning, planning, and using evidence. Tasks are more complex and abstract, often requiring multiple steps, and may involve multiple possible answers or approaches. In Level 3, the math task may be, "Cameron has 8 apples and needs to fill baskets with an equal number of apples. How many baskets should he use if he wants the most apples per basket?" This task demands strategic thinking and an understanding of multiple methods or the reasoning behind the chosen method.

DOK Level 4: Extended Thinking The most complex level, DOK Level 4, involves complex reasoning, planning, and thinking over extended periods of time. Tasks may require students to connect multiple ideas and process information from various sources. For example, consider this Level 4 math task: "Cameron has a number of apples each day and always wants to fill baskets with exactly 4 apples. How many apples could he have to ensure the baskets have exactly 4 apples? What strategy did you use to determine how many apples he could have? What is always true about the total number of apples? Explain how you know this is always true." This task requires extended thinking, generalization of concepts, and application to various scenarios, which is much different from the reproduction and recall of tasks in DOK level 1.

Universal Design for Learning in Mathematics Instruction (K-5)

DOK Levels 3 and 4 comprise cognitively demanding tasks that encourage students to develop and apply mathematical models and strategies in complex, real-world contexts. In a math class designed with a UDL lens, all students are provided access and the opportunity to meaningfully engage with such tasks in order to practice problem-solving and model mathematical thinking. It is critical to proactively build scaffolds and supports into your instruction to meet the needs of all students (Secada et al., 2017). The following strategies incorporate UDL practices to ensure that each student, regardless of their learning needs, can access and engage with the math problem effectively and learn to think in a more complex way:

- **Use multiple representations.** Incorporating multiple representations is crucial for helping all students understand complex problems. For example, you could provide diagrams or visual aids in addition to the verbal or textual description of Cameron's task. A picture showing apples and baskets can help students visualize the problem, aiding those who learn better through visual cues. Providing concrete materials, like counters or actual apples and baskets, can also be beneficial. Physically manipulating these items to solve the problem can help students who excel in hands-on learning or struggle with abstract concepts. This approach deepens the understanding of the problem by linking it to tangible objects.

- **Remove language barriers.** Language can often be a barrier to understanding and solving math problems, especially for students with language processing difficulties or for multilingual learners. To address this, eliminate unnecessary language obstacles and anticipate words that may be confusing (i.e., words with multiple meanings). Providing a glossary is a helpful strategy here. This glossary could clarify terms like *basket* or *group*, ensuring that all students understand the problem's context and requirements.

- **Use contexts that provide real-life sense-making opportunities.** Contextualizing math problems in real-life scenarios can significantly enhance students' comprehension and interest. When students can relate a math problem to their everyday experiences or interests, it becomes more engaging and meaningful to them. For example, you could frame dividing apples into baskets in a context that is familiar to students, such as sharing snacks during class activities or organizing classroom materials. Additionally, tailoring problems to include elements of students' interests, like sports or hobbies, can further enhance engagement. This approach makes the math problem more relatable and demonstrates the practical application of mathematical concepts in everyday life.

Collaborative learning is a powerful way to provide real-life sense-making opportunities. Having students work in groups to solve problems like Cameron's can lead to richer discussions and a deeper understanding of mathematical concepts. In group settings, students can share and learn from one another's perspectives and strategies. To ensure active participation from all group members, assigning specific roles—such as counter, recorder, and strategy checker—can be effective. This not only keeps all members engaged but also allows them to contribute according to their strengths. Collaborative learning fosters a sense of community in the classroom, where students support and learn from one another.

Blended Learning Highlight

Sometimes teachers find it challenging to maintain an organized classroom environment when implementing a high degree of flexibility in teaching methods. Blended learning not only supports deep mathematical understanding and incorporates UDL but also allows teachers to provide focused feedback, support student reflection, and tailor instruction to individual needs.

One blended model is the playlist, which provides students, in pairs or small groups, with tasks to work through. Catlin Tucker, a dear friend and the queen of blended learning, shares that a playlist is a highly effective blended learning model that empowers students to take ownership of their learning as they work toward specific learning objectives at their own pace (Tucker, 2023). The following playlist is an example of a partner playlist that you can design for students to lean into math practices while solving authentic problems.

Playlist Step	Instructions
Skill Practice With Online Resources	Choose a game or app from the options in Google Classroom. Take turns with your partner to solve the challenges you face. You must work together to solve at least four problems. Discuss each challenge and the strategy you used to overcome it. What was the same and what was different about your approaches to the problem?
Pair Practice	Open your green folder to access the multiplication and division problems. There is also a digital copy of the problems in Google Classroom. Read or listen to each problem carefully. Talk with your partner about different ways you could solve the problem and agree on a solution. Remember, two heads are better than one! Options: ★ Use objects like counters or blocks to help build or visualize the situations. ★ Draw pictures or diagrams to help understand and solve the problems. ★ Represent the situations using numbers and symbols. Once you complete the problems, check in with me to share your thinking and I will share the self-evaluation form with each of you to complete individually.

Playlist Step	Instructions
Self-Evaluation	Review the self-assessment. Be honest with yourself. This is a chance to think about what you did well and what you could do better next time when working with a partner to solve problems. Options: ★ Write down what you think went well and what could be improved. ★ Record your thoughts using a voice recorder. ★ Create a simple comic strip or drawing that shows what you learned and how you worked together.

This partner playlist exemplifies how to integrate math practices within a structured framework, encouraging students to tackle real-world problems through collaborative efforts. By integrating options at each step, such as utilizing tangible objects or visual aids for problem-solving and offering varied self-evaluation methods, we adhere to the principles of UDL and enrich the learning experience, ensuring it is accessible and engaging for all students.

Supporting a Nurturing Environment

Creating and supporting a nurturing environment entails proactively building relationships and fostering a space where students feel emotionally and intellectually invested, which is critical for deep, meaningful learning to occur. This involves establishing norms and expectations that value diversity, communicate high expectations, encourage collaboration, and promote a growth mindset. An environment where students' ideas and contributions are valued enables a collaborative, respectful community with a shared purpose in mathematics to emerge (Gutiérrez, 2012).

Math equity research emphasizes this need to nurture belonging and connection among students. Lisa Delpit's book *"Multiplication Is for White People": Raising Expectations for Other People's Children* (2012) discusses the impact of these relationships on students from marginalized backgrounds. Delpit argues that fostering high expectations and nurturing relationships are pivotal to the success of marginalized students. When educators genuinely try to understand and connect with their students' cultural backgrounds and life experiences, it significantly and positively influences learner engagement and achievements in mathematics.

Cobb and Krownapple (2019) add to Delpit's work in their book *Belonging Through a Culture of Dignity*, where they warn educators of "dignity distortions" that undermine students' sense of dignity and belonging in classrooms. Dignity distortions include stereotyping, lack of representation in curriculum materials, limited access to resources and advanced coursework, and cultural insensitivity. We know that underrepresenting diverse racial groups in math education and textbooks can negatively affect student performance. In a study on women, minorities, and persons with disabilities in science and engineering, the National Center for Science and Engineering Statistics (NCSES) found that underrepresented racial groups are less likely to pursue careers in STEM and highlighted that women and leaders of diverse ethnicities are underrepresented in STEM fields. This is partly due to the lack of representation of diverse racial groups in STEM fields, including in math education and program resources (NCSES, 2023).

Consider the following case study and how it highlights dignity distortions. How would a professional learning community (PLC) meeting with a culture like this influence classroom dynamics for diverse learners?

> In an elementary PLC, teachers gather to prepare for an upcoming unit on adding and subtracting two-digit numbers. As they delve into planning, some teachers express concerns about the

accessibility of math word problems with diverse names. To make the problems more accessible, they propose changing the names to more commonly used ones, inadvertently suggesting that students' diverse names are problematic. One teacher comments, "I can't even pronounce those!" Another teacher adds, "It's just easier this way."

The intervention teacher and special educator are both involved in this PLC. One teacher comments to the special educator, "Your kids won't get this unit—can you pull them to do something else?" Another teacher adds, "Yeah, my low kids really struggle with subtraction. I don't want the rest of the class to slow down for them."

One of the main contexts used throughout this unit revolves around collections of seashells. However, the school is located in the middle of a city where many students have never seen the ocean or visited a beach with seashells.

Finally, the teachers assign homework requiring students to bring in supplies from home to practice counting collections as a means to connect to part–whole relationships. The intention is for students to have math manipulatives that remind them of home, which assumes that all students have similar resources, potentially perpetuating inequities.

As you reflect on this case study, it's crucial to examine your own teaching practices and beliefs and consider how they may influence the creation of a nurturing environment free of dignity distortions. As we have shared throughout this chapter, creating a rigorous and inclusive math classroom goes beyond instructional resources; educators must foster a learning environment where all students can express their thoughts and engage in higher-level thinking and problem-solving in a community of belonging.

We all carry a blend of visible and invisible identities that help us define who we are as human beings. Among these held identities is how we see ourselves as mathematicians. *Math identity* refers to an individual's sense of self, beliefs, attitudes, and confidence in relation to mathematics and their own mathematical abilities.

When we use our knowledge and understanding of our own identities and our students' identities to proactively design our instruction, we can more readily design high-quality, equity-based learning opportunities for our students as we intentionally honor their humanity. This is especially imperative when we consider our students who hold identities that have been historically marginalized based on race, class, ethnicity, gender, and sexual orientation. Understanding intersectional identities helps teachers recognize the diverse experiences and perspectives that students bring to the mathematics classroom. We must affirm all of our students' diverse identities while holding high expectations for them if we seek to create a math classroom intentionally designed for all students (Aguirre et al., 2013).

REFLECTION QUESTIONS

1. How does the "do it like me" approach in math education mirror the curse of Echo in Greek mythology? Discuss the implications of this approach on students' ability to express and develop their unique mathematical understanding.

2. Based on Lisa Delpit's work and your own experiences, discuss the role of nurturing relationships between educators and students in the context of math education. How do these relationships impact students' engagement, motivation, and academic success, especially for students from diverse backgrounds?

3. How can the integration of real-life contexts and culturally responsive pedagogies enhance the relevance and accessibility of mathematics for your students?

4. In what ways can you balance the use of standardized materials with the need to adapt instruction to meet the diverse needs of your students, ensuring both fidelity to curriculum and integrity in delivery?

3

Growing Positive Mathematical Mindsets for Teachers and Students

Igniting Your Inner Math Person

Picture this—you're at a summer music festival, lounging on a blanket with your besties. Your friend, who works as a contractor for a local business, joins you to catch up. As you share stories, you mention, "I'm reading this book about UDL and math," and he responds, chuckling while stacking snacks on his napkin, "Ugh, that sounds rough—I'm totally not a math person."

It's a sentiment you've heard too often, but depending on the context, you sometimes delve deeper. In this case, you ask, "Oh, really? You're a contractor, right? When was the last time you measured something to the nearest quarter inch or figured out how much material you needed for a space?" After briefly pausing, he admits, "Well, multiple times today, obviously."

Sipping your cocktail and relaxing back on the blanket, you say, "See? You are a math person. We all are." This interaction highlights a crucial point—many people use math in everyday activities without recognizing it, an insight beautifully illuminated in the context of UDL principles applied to math education.

Unhelpful beliefs in a lack of perceived ability, perpetuated by those who are successful in the current design of our education system, have led many educators to believe they can't apply UDL to math. When teachers expect that math will be too difficult for them or their students to learn and understand, they contribute to the inevitability of their lack of success. John Hattie's meta-analysis of influences on student achievement encourages us to consider the impact on student learning based on *effect size*, a measure for comparing the relationship of two variables across content and over time. Hattie specifies the hinge point for identifying what is and is not effective for student learning as d = 0.40. Teacher expectations resulted in a 0.43 effect size, while teacher–student relationships resulted in a 0.72 effect size. Developing high expectations for each student resulted in an effect size of 1.44. Thus, we can conclude that the relationship between holding high expectations and positive outcomes is strong (Hattie, 2012).

Our systems must support teachers in seeing that their decision-making impacts student learning. We need teachers to believe that achievement is alterable and they can enable learning in their classrooms for every single student (Hattie, 2012). To implement UDL effectively, it may be helpful to envision it as a three-legged stool (Novak, 2022), as shown in Figure 3.1.

The strength of a three-legged stool lies in its inherent stability and balance, achieved through the distribution of forces. When weight is applied to the top of the stool, the three legs spread the load evenly and support one another, preventing any single leg from bearing the entire burden. This ensures that the stool remains steady and can withstand varying pressures from different directions.

The three-legged stool is a powerful analogy for creating successful, inclusive, and humanizing learning spaces in

Beliefs   System drivers   Skill sets

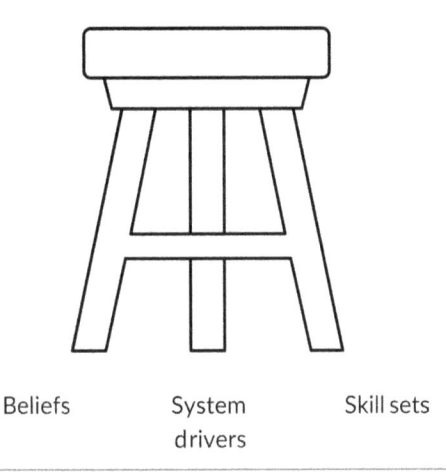

Figure 3.1. The three-legged stool is a powerful analogy for creating successful, inclusive, and humanizing learning spaces in mathematics.

mathematics. Each leg represents a critical element—beliefs, skill sets, and system drivers—and the stool would topple if one of these were missing. Likewise, transforming a classroom, school, or district requires all three legs to be solidly in place to ensure a stable foundation for growth and progress.

Let's delve deeper into the significance of each leg. The belief system represents teachers' core convictions about their students' abilities and potential, as well as about their own efficacy. This involves recognizing and challenging any limiting beliefs that might hinder the implementation of effective instructional practices. For instance, when teachers say, "I can't apply UDL to math," it is essential for them to then ask, "Is what I believe empowering or disempowering me from creating the learning environment I want for myself and my students?" Addressing and reshaping these beliefs can pave the way for a more flexible and accommodating teaching approach.

The second leg, skill sets, encompasses the toolbox of instructional techniques, methods, and knowledge that educators possess.

Think of this leg as the Swiss Army knife of teaching. A robust skill set is indispensable for designing instruction that meets the diverse needs of our students, who require support in various academic, behavioral, social-emotional, and linguistic aspects. To make things even more complex, student needs are dynamic and continuously evolving, making teaching an ever-changing landscape. What works effectively one day may not yield the same results the next. Ongoing professional development opportunities that empower teachers with evidence-based practices and innovative teaching approaches are critical to fortifying this leg.

The third leg, the system drivers, refers to the organizational structures, policies, and practices that support and reinforce effective teaching and learning. A comprehensive, multi-tiered system of support ensures that the school or district operates cohesively, with a shared vision and common goals. It involves providing the necessary high-quality instructional materials, innovative technology, and strong leadership support to enable teachers to implement evidence-based practices successfully. When the system drivers are robust, they create an environment conducive to growth and progress.

To illustrate the interdependence of these three legs, consider a scenario in which a teacher faces challenges implementing UDL in math based on limiting beliefs about their own or their students' efficacy. Such self-doubt weakens this leg of the stool. As a result, a teacher may hesitate to explore new instructional approaches, sticking to more traditional methods that may feel safer but are not as effective for all students. However, by recognizing and addressing these disempowering beliefs, the teacher can build a stronger foundation for UDL implementation.

Table 3-1 shares questions to both reflect on as a teacher and ask your students as you start to disrupt any current unhelpful beliefs around self-efficacy in math class and address barriers to access.

Table 3-1: Reflecting on Beliefs About Self-Efficacy in Math Class (All Learners Network, 2023)

For Classroom Teachers	★ What does your planning process look like for math? ★ How do you typically use your math instructional minutes? ★ What materials do you use from your program? ★ What other materials do you use? ★ How do students access the math tools or materials in your classroom? ★ What assessments feel the most useful to you? ★ How do you know what your students know? How do you use this information collectively to make instructional decisions? ★ Are all students showing growth? How do you know? ★ What supports are in place for students not showing growth? ★ What do you do when you identify gaps in understanding? ★ What does intervention support look like in math for students in your class? ★ What would help make you a better math instructor?
For Special Educators	★ How is your support for students designed across the day? ★ What does collaboration look like with classroom teachers? ★ How do you modify core lesson materials for students? ★ What materials do you use to support students with IEP goals? ★ How do your students get access to grade-level materials? ★ How do your students get access to just-right practice materials? ★ What would help make you a better math instructor?
For Support Staff	★ How do the students you support feel about math? ★ Why do you think they feel that way? ★ How do you support students during math? ★ How effective does your support feel? ★ What would help make you a better support to students?

Table 3-1 Continued. Reflecting on Beliefs About Self-Efficacy in Math Class (All Learners Network, 2023)

For Coaches and Interventionists	★ How does your role help to support teachers (students) teaching math? ★ What is the goal of your interactions with teachers (students)? ★ Where have you been successful working with teachers (students)? ★ What are the barriers to reaching your goal(s)? ★ If you could change something in the system, what would that be?
For Students	★ How do you feel about math? ★ What does math work look like in your classroom? ★ When do you feel like you can share your ideas in math class? ★ What do you do when you don't know the answer? ★ Do you work with partners, by yourself, or with groups of other students during math? ★ When do you get the opportunity to think in math class?

We are asking you to become aware of your beliefs about your competence in teaching and learning math. Although our society commonly uses unhelpful labels like "math person" or "not a math person," it is important to recognize that *who* we classify as a math person depends entirely on *how* we define a math person. The truth is that everyone is a math person, and everyone has a math brain. Our responsibility is to listen to and celebrate the creative ways students approach problems to ensure that they all see the brilliance in their thinking and ideas.

Belief in Your Self-Efficacy

As we seek to build a sense of belonging in math class, we must explore our held assumptions about ourselves as mathematicians.

It takes courage to be vulnerable and name our discomfort with the doing and teaching of mathematics. Many of our earliest experiences in the classroom left us feeling "less than" or incapable of doing math—but remember, there's no "math brain" and no "math gene." All of us are mathematicians, but somewhere along the way, we told ourselves otherwise.

To shift your pedagogical practice in teaching mathematics, you need to examine your beliefs in your self-efficacy. You have the greatest impact on student learning because you have the opportunity to design the learning experiences for your students. So, start by asking yourself:

- How did I learn math? Was it a positive or negative experience?
- Who was included in my math classes? Who was excluded?
- What beliefs do I hold about who a mathematician is? Do I see myself represented in those beliefs?

Support Positive Math Mindsets for Our Students

By cultivating a safe and flexible learning space where students feel valued and supported, we enhance their motivation to actively participate in mathematical discussions and problem-solving, making the learning experience more enjoyable and meaningful for everyone involved. Dr. Tyrone Howard, a professor of education in the School of Education & Information Studies at UCLA, described the impact of belonging in the math classroom in his keynote address at the NCSM Leadership in Math Education National Conference in September 2022. He emphasized that a lack of belonging saps concentration and focus. It is *our* responsibility to have a relationship with our students.

As educators and leaders, we must reflect on the messages we communicate, the experiences we offer, and the relationships we cultivate to ensure every student experiences a sense of belonging in our classrooms and views themselves as capable mathematicians. It is vital for students to feel connected—to believe they are an integral part of the classroom community—to facilitate their learning, as research is clear that students who feel a sense of connection with their peers are more likely to achieve positive academic results (Oyserman et al., 2006).

Payton's Story: Overcoming Challenges in Math Learning

At the beginning of the school year, Ashley was provided with insights about the incoming third-grade students. Among them was Payton, a student who, according to his second-grade teachers, harbored negative beliefs about his learning abilities. These teachers had fixed mindsets regarding Payton's potential and shared them with Ashley.

In the initial days of school, Ashley led sharing circles to delve into students' needs, interests, and academic perceptions. A particularly telling activity gauged students' views of their capabilities in math. Payton's response was a sheet filled with scribbles and the words "I HATE THIS" boldly marked across it. His discomfort with math was further evident as he would often roll on the floor, tip over chairs, or talk over instructions during math sessions.

Recognizing the urgent need to shift Payton's outlook and foster a supportive learning environment, Ashley used strategies to build trust, offer choices, and reinforce his belief in his own abilities. It was also vital for the class to understand the importance of every student's voice in this math community. Ashley set a specific goal for Payton: to stay engaged for the first five minutes of math class, with the freedom to take a short break afterward if he needed. This plan was clearly communicated with Payton, emphasizing the value of his contributions to the class's math discussions.

Despite these efforts, success was not immediate. Payton continued to disengage quickly, challenging Ashley's belief in his capability to meet even this initial goal. This situation prompted her to reflect more deeply on creating a sense of safety, belonging, and interest for Payton in the math classroom.

The breakthrough came from connecting math to something Payton loved: fast cars. Initiating class with an activity featuring sports cars like the Bugatti Chiron Super Sport and the Hennessey Venom grabbed his attention. Payton engaged by comparing their acceleration rates—a topic he was passionate about. Ashley repeated this approach with various car-related math problems, which gradually helped Payton stay engaged for longer periods.

Over the year, Payton's time spent engaged in math class increased from the initial 5 minutes up to about 20 minutes. This was a significant improvement, considering he had missed over 95% of his math instruction in previous years.

Students decide in the first five minutes of class whether they will engage or check out. When they believe they do not belong, feel undervalued, or perceive themselves as incapable of engaging, they often physically or mentally abandon the class. This can manifest as zoning out, creating distractions, or exhibiting unexpected behaviors. Sometimes, this leads them to actually leave the room or cause a disruption significant enough that they are told to leave. Starting our lessons with welcoming, inclusive tasks that are "low floor, high ceiling" with multiple entry points allows students to see themselves as essential members of the learning community (CASEL, 2024). Low-floor, high-ceiling tasks provide rich math experiences to all students. These tasks allow for multiple strategies and models, invite all students to engage, lend themselves to natural extensions, and encourage explanation and justification.

In math class, we encourage all educators to use a *launch* or a *number sense* routine daily in the first 5 to 15 minutes of a balanced math block for purposeful, discussion-rich learning opportunities. The purpose of this time is to encourage all students to engage in the math lesson for the day at the very beginning of the math block (Lang, 2016). Launch math tasks could practice, strengthen, or introduce new mathematical ideas and should be engaging and open-ended enough that all students can participate.

"Which One Doesn't Belong?" (WODB) is a particular type of launch activity where students are presented with a set of four items (these can be numbers, shapes, graphs, or any mathematical objects—like sports cars, in Payton's case!) and asked to identify which item does not belong with the others and, most importantly, why. The beauty of WODB is that there's no single correct answer; any item might not belong, depending on the criteria the student chooses to apply. If you're interested in launching lessons with the WODB strategy, visit https://wodb.ca.

For example, in Figure 3.2, some students might say 9 doesn't belong because it is a single-digit number. Others may say 43

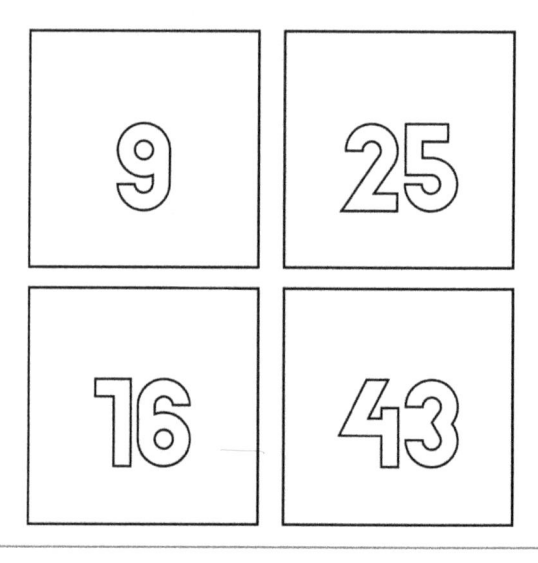

Figure 3.2: A Which One Doesn't Belong activity

doesn't belong because it is the only prime number. Some may notice 9 doesn't belong because the digits do not add up to 7.

Some students might find a reason only for one of the choices, whereas other students may find multiple reasons for each. As you can imagine from Figure 3.2, the launch provides opportunities for dialogue between and among peers. This is critical in the first five minutes because it conveys that all voices matter and all students' ideas are valued in the math learning community. If we believe (and we do!) that all students can learn math well, we must ensure they see that in themselves in the first five minutes of math class.

Returning to our story about Payton: After a few years, he and his family decided to seek an alternative education setting. Before transitioning to a new school, Payton wanted to spend extra time engaging in math activities in the math coaching office. Although he did not master every concept by the end of third grade, he left with a fundamental understanding that he was capable of learning and that there were people who believed in his potential. This experience underscores the importance of tailored educational approaches and the profound impact of believing in each student's ability to succeed.

Positioning Students as Competent

Presuming competence is giving all students the benefit of the doubt and believing they are capable of high levels of success (Biklen & Burke, 2006). In math, it means you believe that every single student has the potential to develop their thinking, learning, and understanding of mathematics. This presumption is critical if we seek to create inclusive math classrooms that promote deep learning of mathematical content for every child. In a seminal publication about presuming competence, Biklen and Burke share the following:

> There needs to be a strong commitment to inclusive education that expects student agency, where the participation of the

student in the heart of the classroom is a given, not an experiment and not conditional, and where participation amounts to more than mere physical presence; the student must be seen as someone more than a body to fill the chair. Only then is the stage set for an attitude of problem solving where, when difficulties arise, teachers, teaching consultants, parents, and administrators can work with the child to figure out solutions. Good teaching involves dialogue with the student, for teachers cannot assume they know what students are thinking or aspiring to. (p.172)

Both of us are struck by the power of this statement. Our students dream of success, and we don't have the power or the privilege to take away their opportunities to experience success and feel a deep sense of belonging. To learn more about presuming competence, we recommend watching a seven-minute YouTube video called "The Importance of Presuming Competence" from the brilliant Shelley Moore (Five Moore Minutes, 2021). There is another concept related to presuming competence that resonates deeply: the least dangerous assumption.

Presuming incompetence or creating learning environments where students do not experience competence is dangerous and comes at a significant cost to our learners. The alternative—believing in students and presuming competence in our learners and ourselves, known as making the "least dangerous assumption" (Donnellan, 1984)—is a powerful tool for educational equity, ensuring that our pedagogical choices support the most positive outcomes for students. It shifts the focus from a deficit-based model, which looks at what students cannot do, to a strength-based model that builds on what students *can* do and recognizes that their potential is often untapped or unseen because of inappropriate or inflexible teaching methods. Teachers' mindsets, particularly their belief in students' capacity to learn, directly impact student outcomes and can significantly influence learning math well (Hattie, 2012). Teachers can support students to build a growth mindset—a belief in their own potential to learn and improve—to promote positive learning outcomes (Dweck, 2008).

This is more than just telling students they are capable. We have seen countless classrooms where teachers post motivational posters on the wall, refer to students as brilliant scholars, and try to help learners see themselves as mathematicians and problem solvers (Gutiérrez, 2012). But positioning students as competent entails educators acknowledging and publicly championing the intellectual contributions of every single one of their students (Hattie, 2012).

We believe there's a genuine desire among teachers to position students as competent. Yet there's often a hesitation to express it publicly, maybe because they haven't seen tangible evidence of this competence yet. This dilemma echoes the insights of Jean Anyon in her groundbreaking article "Social Class and the Hidden Curriculum of Work" (1980). Anyon's concept of the "hidden curriculum" sheds light on how teachers' expectations are implicitly communicated through their instructional methods and the criteria they use to define student success. Her work highlights the subtle yet profound ways teacher expectations and beliefs can influence the instruction they deliver to students. Recognizing the existence and impact of this hidden curriculum is the first step; educators must confront their beliefs about student competence to truly position students as competent. Take a moment to pause and reflect on the following questions:

- When I assign tasks, am I challenging every student, or am I subconsciously making them easier for those I perceive as less capable?
- Am I consistently providing opportunities for all students to demonstrate their understanding in diverse ways beyond traditional testing methods, or am I asking students to echo what I have taught them?
- How do I react when a student struggles? Do I view it as a natural part of the learning process and an opportunity

for growth, or as a confirmation of preconceived notions about their abilities?

- Am I using language like "They can't do that," "They won't do that," or "They are the low kids," when talking with others about my students?

Now, you may be thinking, what about students who really struggle? Those who have a modified curriculum or haven't been successful yet? Indeed, this is the crux of the problem. Research continually affirms that all students, including those with significant intellectual disabilities, are capable of learning mathematics. It's not about *if* they can learn but about *how* they can be taught in ways that resonate with their learning needs.

A study by Jitendra et al. (2013) argues that instruction designed to meet the diverse needs of students leads to significant improvements in mathematical problem-solving skills, including among students with learning disabilities. As educators, our task is not to question whether students with intellectual disabilities can learn mathematics but to continuously innovate and adapt our teaching strategies to unlock the potential in every student, recognizing and valuing their capacity for mathematical thinking and positioning them as competent. We support a positive math identity when our students see themselves as being fully capable of doing math and know that others also perceive them that way.

Building Your Conceptual Understanding

For many of us, mathematics teaching and learning today look drastically different from our own experiences as students. Changes in the teaching and learning of mathematics are focused on two key levers: math content knowledge and pedagogy. The rest of this book is structured to address a bit of both. Each chapter is focused on a critical mathematical concept that all teachers of students in that grade band should understand. Interwoven are math teaching practices, aligned with the UDL Guidelines, that support equitable access to grade-level mathematics for all students. Our students need to learn math by connecting one concept to another and recognizing which concepts build over time.

Teachers and students need to understand how subitizing (the cognitive process that allows us to recognize how many objects are in a small set without counting) impacts both additive and multiplicative understanding. They need to grasp how the concept of number composition and decomposition, introduced as early as preK, continues to build over time as they work with fractions and solve algebraic equations. As you explore the following chapters, consider areas of new learning to dive into as both a learner and teacher of mathematics. *You* are a mathematician. You deserve opportunities to know, do, and think about mathematics, and we hope the following chapters provide you with the opportunity to do so.

REFLECTION QUESTIONS

1. The chapter's three-legged stool analogy emphasizes the interconnectedness of belief systems, skill sets, and system drivers in implementing UDL effectively. Reflect on the significance of each leg and how all three contribute to transforming math classrooms into inclusive spaces where all students can thrive.

2. Consider the shift in your own mindset as a knower and doer of mathematics. What were your experiences like as a student? As a teacher?

3. Build your own conceptual understanding by solving and discussing the following tasks with your professional learning teams. After you solve the tasks, share your strategies. What are the similarities and differences between

your approaches? What was your initial response to "We are doing some math today"?

- **Task 1:** The Silver Dragons defeated the Robots in the middle school championship basketball game. The Silver Dragons scored 87 points. Find at least one potential combination of 3-, 2-, and 1-point baskets that the Silver Dragons could have made.

- **Task 2:** Katie loves to run long distances in her free time. She hopes to run 36 miles by the end of the week. She will spend time running around her local high school each day. Each lap around the school is $\frac{2}{3}$ mile. How many laps does she need to run to complete her goal?

- **Task 3:** Marcus is trying to save enough money to buy a new gaming console that costs $270. He earns an allowance of $9 per week from his parents. In addition, Marcus mows his neighbor's lawn every two weeks for $8 per mow. How many weeks will it take for Marcus to earn enough to buy the gaming console?

4

Cultivating Early Numeracy Skills

Counting, Sorting, and Organizing

If you've ever listened to Noah Kahan's hit song "Stick Season," you've heard that term used to describe the landscape of Vermont in late October and early November.

> And I love Vermont, but it's the season of the sticks
> And I saw your mom, she forgot that I existed.

As stick season approaches in New England, we wake up to darkness and leave work as a chilly twilight sets in and street lamps turn on. We go to bed earlier because there isn't much to do after 6 p.m. Red, orange, and yellow leaves float whimsically through the air until the late fall rain and wind push the last of them to the ground, leaving behind trees with bare sticks and branches.

The season of the sticks for our New England–born kids is when they finally pull up the remaining annual flowers. For them, it's a time to play in and tear apart the garden beds we meticulously nurtured all summer. This year, Ashley's kids got creative!

As they pulled out the remaining chrysanthemum and aster buds, they bubbled with math-citement (yep, we made that word up!).

"Mom, come look at what we made! It's math in the garden!" Ashley's little loves (ages six and three) explained that they had organized the flower heads in different ways. First, they sorted by color. Then, they sorted by size and shape. Finally, they used four different flower heads to create a "Which One Doesn't Belong?" activity (see Figure 4.1).

Figure 4.1. Organizing flower heads

From the destruction of a garden to a sequence of math talks, stick season—although dark, damp, and cold—reminds us that early numeracy concepts are all around us.

Clear Goals

Early childhood and elementary mathematics provides the foundation for a conceptual understanding of math that builds skills and more complex understanding over time. Its importance cannot be underestimated: Children's early mathematical knowledge has been identified as a predictor of later success in mathematics, even into high school (Claessens et al., 2009). In addition, rich and supportive experiences with early mathematics help children gain critical skills necessary for school and career success. PreK and kindergarten-age students who engage in frequent math explorations begin to understand that they use math every day as they make meaning of their world (Clements & Sarama, 2014). Mathematics helps children organize, classify, compare, create, and make generalizations about their world.

For preK and kindergarten students, the key priority is building conceptual understanding and skill-based competence in counting and number values to 10. This includes the following:

- Rote counting
- Subitizing
- Forward and backward sequence
- 1:1 correspondence
- Cardinality
- Conservation of number

When these students have a strong understanding of number values up to 10, they can more readily build their ability to compose and decompose numbers—the foundation for additive reasoning.

Early Number Values

By exploring the following examples, we can see how a strong grasp of basic number values sets the stage for more advanced numerical concepts and additive reasoning (Fosnot & Dolk, 2001):

- **Rote counting:** Recite numbers in the correct order, both forward and backward, starting at any given number.

    1, 2, 3, 4, 5 . . .

    9, 8, 7, 6 . . .

- **Subitizing:** Instantly recognize the number of objects in a group without counting them.

    "I see 5 circles!"

    "I see 4 and 3, so 7 circles!"

- **Forward and backward sequencing:** Know the forward and backward sequence of numbers using the counting patterns of words and symbols; this includes the ability to name the number that comes before a given number as well as the one that comes after.

    "2 comes before 3 . . ."

    "6 comes after 5 . . ."

Cultivating Early Numeracy Skills

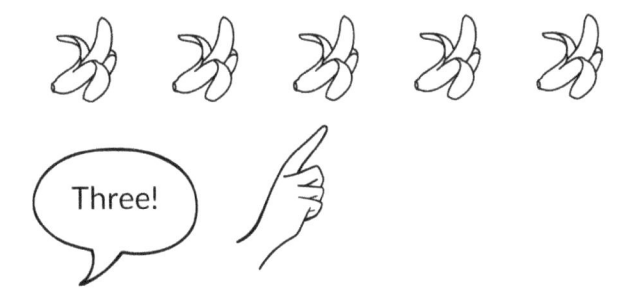

- **1:1 correspondence:** Count a group of objects by assigning one number to each object and counting each object only once.
- **Cardinality:** Understand that the last number used to count a group of objects represents how many are in the group.
- **Conservation of number:** Understand that the number of objects in a collection does not change if the collection is moved around or spread out.

Arrangement 1

Arrangement 2

- **Number values to 10:** Understand that digits up to 10 represent a value or number of items.

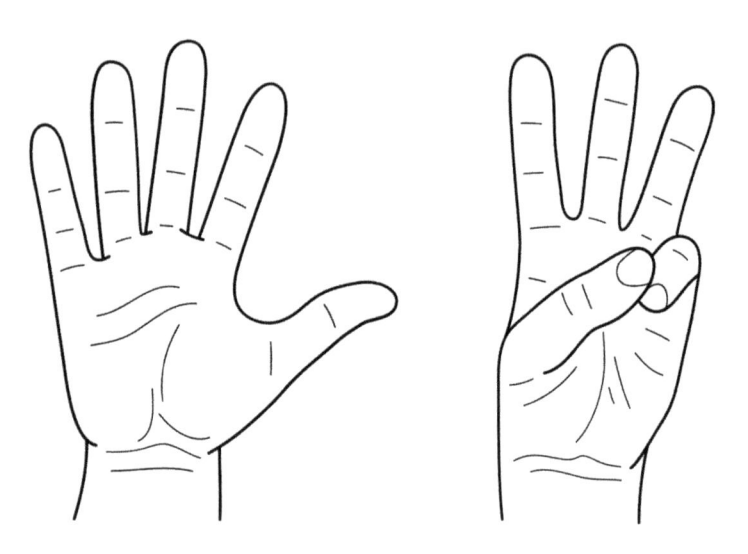

There are 8 fingers showing, meaning there are 8 individual fingers to build up to the value of 8.

From Traditional Math to Sense-Making Opportunities

As we discussed earlier in the book, traditional math instruction focuses on memorizing procedures. However, students also need practice in critical thinking, productive struggle, revising previous ideas, and sense-making. UCLA professor of psychology Dr. James Stigler shares, "We teach math as disconnected facts and as a series of steps or procedures—do this, and this and this—without connecting procedures with concepts, and without thinking or problem-solving" (Wolpert, 2018). When we consider the strengths and needs of our youngest students, we must help them make this procedure-to-concept connection if we expect all students to learn math well.

The National Council of Teachers of Mathematics (NCTM) identifies critical improvements to our math instructional landscape, including

- prioritizing the development of deep conceptual understanding so that children experience joy and confidence in themselves as emerging mathematicians;
- dismantling structural obstacles that stand in the way of mathematics working for each and every student;
- implementing equitable instructional practices to cultivate students' positive mathematical identities and a strong sense of agency; and
- organizing mathematics along a common pathway grounded in the use of mathematical practices and processes to coherently develop a strong foundation of deep mathematical understanding for each and every child (Huinker, 2020).

Consider the story about Ashley's kids playing in the garden. Seeing the joy of math in the real world is critical for our emerging mathematicians as we help build their positive math identities. This includes presenting opportunities for them to solve math tasks, both independently and collaboratively, that are relevant to their real lives. It requires students to share and compare their thinking with others and model their strategy for solving with concrete and visual tools. They need access to learning opportunities that require reasoning and sense-making. In short, "children should be positioned with the authority to draw upon their resources (e.g., strategies, tools, and prior experiences) to explore and discuss tasks and delve deeper into the mathematics" (Huinker, 2020).

Mr. Aguilar's story is an excellent example of a classroom teacher proactively designing the math learning environment for his students with both the UDL framework and quality math teaching practices in mind.

Mr. Aguilar Counting Collections

Mr. Aguilar's kindergarten class is reading the story *Grandma's Purse* by Vanessa Brantley-Newton. This charming story celebrates the relationship between a granddaughter and her grandmother. When Grandma Mimi comes to visit, she brings love and treats and, of course, her purse. Her purse is always full of fancy collections and various items. Students can relate to the relationship with an elder friend or family member who always has a bag full of "things"! They are deeply invested in this story, making it an excellent context to build math problems.

Mr. Aguilar: *We have loved reading and talking about* Grandma's Purse! *I've loved hearing your stories about grandparents and friends who carry lots of things in their bags. Today, we will practice counting objects like those found in Grandma Mimi's purse!*

Mr. Aguilar has collections of varying sizes and objects that relate to the items found in Grandma Mimi's purse: lip balm and lipsticks, hairpins, coins, various hard candies, photos, and magazine clippings.

Mr. Aguilar: *I am going to randomly put you in groups of three. Your group will choose one collection to go to first. Your job is to determine how many objects are in the collection. You can access any math tools on the shelf by the carpet. What are some tools that you can use to help count objects?*

Students: *We can make groups, use fives frames or tens frames, and write tally marks!*

Mr. Aguilar: *Okay, here are your groups—let's get started!*

As Mr. Aguilar moves about the room, students are deeply engaged in this task. They have reviewed the tools they can use to help them organize and keep track of their counting. Mr. Aguilar has prepared questions focusing on early numeracy concepts that he can ask as he moves about the room, like "I see you labeled that group 5; how do you know? What if we added one more lip gloss to that pile? How many would we have? Is there a different way you could count this group?" Students have the opportunity to choose which collection they want to focus on. They can then choose to go to a different collection, break their collection into smaller parts, or combine collections to increase the number they are counting. As the work time comes to a close, Mr. Aguilar invites students to share their counting strategies with the class. He ensures that the thinking and strategies remain with the students while naming specific mathematical strategies and tools that they are describing.

Mr. Aguilar: *Oh! I hear you saying that you organized the collection into groups of 2 and then counted each group of 2 to make 6, but I heard Marcus say he filled in his fives frame to count the 5 and then counted 1 more. What's the same about Marcus's strategy and Diana's strategy? What's different?*

Mr. Aguilar reinforces the lesson's goal, ensuring students understand that they are practicing their counting and organizing strategies. He then chooses to extend the lesson, building on this relevant context and allowing students to see math in their daily lives.

Mr. Aguilar: *We really enjoyed counting collections today and practiced important concepts like organizing, counting, and knowing the value of digits. Tomorrow, I'd like to invite you to bring in a collection of objects from your own lives—rocks, cards, or other interesting objects. I will send a note home at the end of the day to ensure folks at home know it's okay to share if you want to! If you don't want to bring anything in, I will have some collections here for you.*

Mr. Aguilar has already communicated this task with caregivers using the mutually agreed-upon communication format. He will also prepare collections of objects from the classroom for students to choose from if they don't bring anything from home.

* * *

Every child must be given learning opportunities to develop a deep understanding of mathematics through challenging tasks, time to explore the mathematics of the tasks, discussing math with other students, and seeking math in the real world. Mr. Aguilar addressed all of these areas.

Before engaging in this math lesson, Mr. Aguilar considered the variability of his students' needs. He proactively identified a context that would be relevant to all students. He considered various options for students to enter this task by preparing different-sized collections and having helpful organizing math tools available for all students to access in a community space. He provided scaffolding by allowing students to brainstorm strategies before getting to work, and promoted math dialogue and collaboration by putting students in random groups of three. Mr. Aguilar also considered what he needed to ensure all students had the opportunity to be challenged in this lesson by preparing questions he could ask as he moved about the space. Finally, Mr. Aguilar ensured students saw and did math in their everyday lives.

Mr. Aguilar leveraged UDL to provide engaging math instruction by selecting a story that resonated with his students' personal experiences. *Grandma's Purse* taps into students' memories and relationships with elder family members, fostering a deep emotional connection that bolsters engagement and motivation. To amplify UDL, students can read the story independently (a great option for early readers!), sit in a small group and listen to the teacher read the story, or access a video reading so they can pause and rewatch. This personalization ensures the learning experience is meaningful for each student. Giving students the autonomy to choose which collection to count further enhances their engagement, as it empowers them with a sense of control and ownership in their learning process. Counting lip glosses is way more fun than counting cubes! As a follow-up, students can bring in their own collections, but it's critical that students who do not participate are not excluded.

Mr. Aguilar's approach helps students develop essential skills such as numeracy (by reviewing number concepts, counting, and recognizing the value of digits); organization (by grouping, sorting, and using tools like fives frames, tens frames, and tally marks); collaboration (by working in groups to solve problems and discuss strategies); critical thinking (by analyzing different counting methods and finding efficient ways to count); and sense-making (by seeing math in real-world objects and experiences). The lesson features a variety of tangible collections, such as lip balms, hairpins, and coins, that relate back to the story. This approach allows students to connect mathematical concepts to real-world objects. The diverse nature of the collections appeals to different interests, ensuring that all students find something that captures their attention. The availability of various counting tools offers students multiple ways to engage and interact with the concept of counting, accommodating their individual strengths and cognitive processing preferences.

The lesson encourages active participation and exploration by allowing students to choose how they count and organize objects. As Mr. Aguilar circulates the room, posing specific questions, he challenges each student at their own level, promoting critical thinking and problem-solving skills. Finally, inviting students to share their counting strategies with the class gives them the opportunity to articulate their mathematical thinking and be recognized for their efforts, which is a great way to integrate social coaching and build collaboration and community.

REFLECTION QUESTIONS

1. How does Mr. Aguilar's use of the story *Grandma's Purse* enhance student engagement in early numeracy, and what other stories or contexts could you use to create an interdisciplinary math lesson?

2. In what ways do the different collections and counting tools in Mr. Aguilar's lesson provide varied means of representation and action, and how could you adapt or expand them for students with diverse learning needs? Reflect on the inclusivity of the tools and materials used, and think about additional or alternative resources you could incorporate to address a wider range of learning preferences and abilities.

3. How does the collaborative aspect of Mr. Aguilar's lesson, where students work in groups and share strategies, contribute to building a community of learners, and what other collaborative activities could further enhance peer learning and mathematical understanding?

4. Considering the principles of UDL, how effectively does Mr. Aguilar's lesson anticipate and address the variability in student learning, and what additional strategies could you employ to ensure even greater inclusivity and engagement?

5

Unlock Access to Additive Reasoning

Penny Candy Overages

North Conway, New Hampshire, is a classic New England village with an old-fashioned train station and a picturesque main street lined with cozy cafes and quaint shops, including Zeb's General Store, which is painted mustard yellow and has a 200-pound stuffed bear sitting on its front porch. If you're ever in the area and need a cold can of Moxie, watercolor diner art, a pickling kit, or a maple product, you know where to go. To this day, Zeb's still has a candy counter with homemade fudge, but you can't get candy for a penny anymore! Oh, to be back when you could.

Imagine the following scenario, which happened to Katie and her little sister, Lindie, when they were finally old enough to hit Zeb's candy counter without supervision. With a dollar in her pocket, Katie obsessively calculated the cost of candy as she added it to her basket, ensuring she stayed within her allowance. Lindie did not. After losing track of her for a while, Katie saw Lindie rushing toward her with a panicked face, exclaiming, "I don't have enough!"

Being the helpful older sister, Katie asked how much Lindie needed, ready to sacrifice her own selections. Combined, their funds were insufficient for the mountain of candy piled on the scale. Later, Katie learned that Lindie's excessive stockpile of wax bottles was intended to fashion makeshift retainers for all her stuffed animals' orthodontic needs.

Lindie, who could have outpaced her classmates in a math fact sprint workshop, found her number sense completely overwhelmed by all the sugary temptations and the pressing orthodontic requirements of her plush patients. The dazzling array of choices and the plans for her imaginative project seemingly short-circuited her ordinarily precise arithmetic skills.

Understanding Additive Reasoning

Many people believe that additive reasoning is primarily about memorizing addition and subtraction facts. Remember all those times tables we memorized in elementary school? All the math sprints where we competed to see who could add and subtract the quickest? Additive reasoning is so much more than that. Don't get us wrong: Knowing math facts can be helpful and support automaticity. But true additive reasoning involves understanding the relationships between numbers and applying this understanding to solve problems.

Research highlights the critical role of additive reasoning in children's mathematical development (Ching & Nunes, 2017). A longitudinal study found that additive reasoning explained a substantial and significant variance in calculation and story problem-solving skills after controlling for age, IQ, and working memory. The researchers argue, "One educational implication of this study is that quantitative reasoning should be a central aspect addressed in mathematics education curricula. Children need to learn to reason about relations between quantities in order to solve problems, not only about arithmetic" (p. 50).

Another misconception is that additive reasoning is relevant only in early elementary education. In reality, additive reasoning forms the foundation for more complex mathematical concepts taught in higher grades, such as algebra, calculus, and beyond. Skills like decomposing numbers, understanding the properties of addition and subtraction, and solving word problems are foundational and remain relevant and important throughout one's mathematical education.

Often, students are taught specific methods or algorithms for solving addition and subtraction problems, leading them to believe that these are the only correct ways to solve such problems. As we shared earlier in the book, this aligns with many teachers' own learned experiences in school, not to mention the lack of preparation in our preservice training programs to support inclusive math teaching practices. Instead, the development of additive reasoning should include flexible thinking and the understanding that there are multiple strategies to arrive at a solution. Encouraging diverse methods, such as using number lines, manipulatives, mental math, or drawing models, fosters a deeper understanding and adaptability in problem-solving.

Key Math Concepts and Models: Additive Reasoning

As students move to first and second grade, they build on the early number concepts they established in preK and kindergarten. Students are learning to apply counting strategies and initial number relationships, including comparing magnitude, one more and one less, anchors to 5 and 10, and the earliest understanding of part to whole. Students explore with manipulatives and models to build their place value understanding within 120 to support their ability to add and subtract fluently. Students are asked to consider tasks that involve making 10 and then "some more." By the end of second grade, students explore the difference in the value of the digit 2 in the ones place compared to the digit 2 in the tens place and 2 in the hundreds place.

When students explore math concepts with visual and concrete models, they have the opportunity to develop reasoning and sense-making. This exploration asks teachers to consider the most effective models to support additive reasoning. One example is *tens frames*, a critical mathematical model that illuminates strategies for making tens, comparing quantities, and adding and subtracting. A tens frame consists of a rectangular frame divided into 2 rows of 5 boxes each, creating 10 boxes (see Figure 5.1). This presentation or framing helps students count, see number relationships, and develop an understanding of base 10 as our place value system (Fosnot & Dolk, 2001).

Starting with the tens frames model, students can explore the big idea that our number system includes the digits 0 through 9, and once we fill that frame, there's no other way to represent the value we get when we have 9 and 1 more than to add another place value; thus, 9 and 1 more is written as 1 in the tens place with 0 more. As students develop confidence and fluency with tens frames, they can use multiple tens frames to build on their understanding of place value within 120. For example, if I have 6 tens frames and 4 of those frames are filled, and the fifth frame has

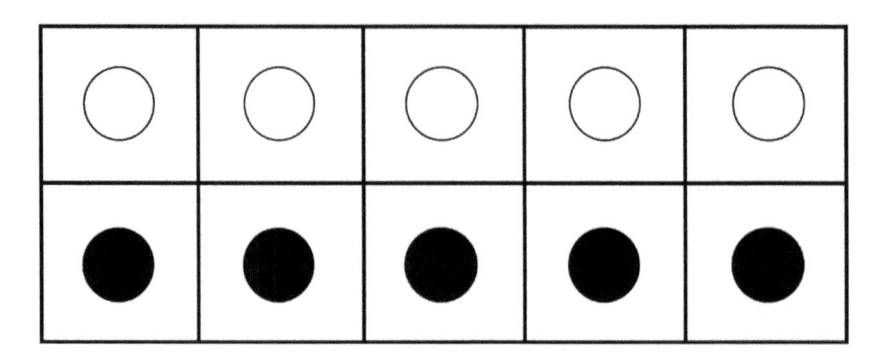

Figure 5.1. A completed tens frame highlighting the two groups of five

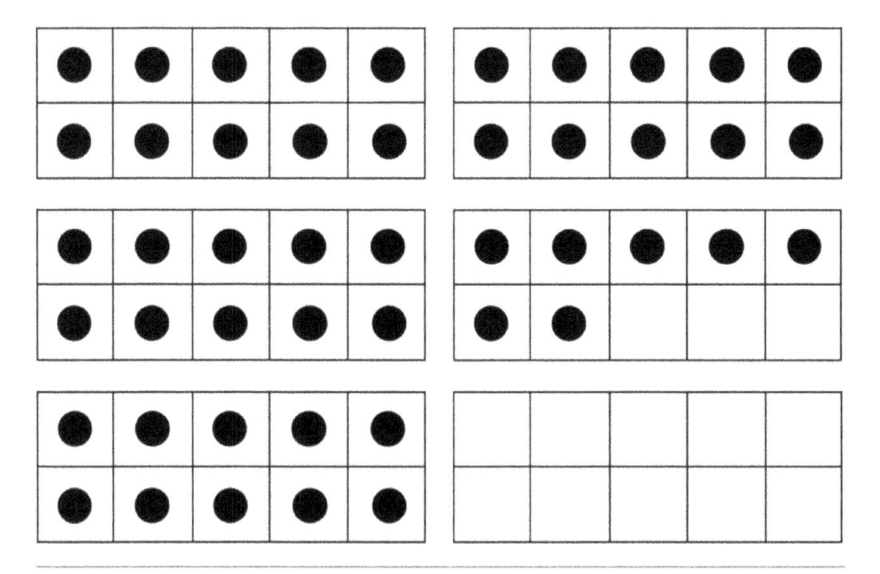

Figure 5.2. Six tens frames: four are complete, one has seven objects, and one is empty.

7 items, we can represent the total value as 4 tens and 7 ones, or 47 (see Figure 5.2).

Students continue to practice counting on and counting back from any given number and can use their tens frames to develop strategies for adding and subtracting within 100.

As students progress through grade 2, they can shift to more abstract models, including an articulated number line. They may not need to physically move objects on the tens frames, and may now see that 10 dashes on a number line are a visual and physical representation of 10 units and then some more. Now, students should be able to build on their strong place value understanding to compose and decompose numbers to add and subtract.

- **Composition:** All numbers are made up of other numbers; students can visualize the numbers inside other numbers first.

7 is composed of 7 ones, or 5 ones and 2 more ones:

38 is composed of 3 tens and 8 ones or 30 and 8 more.

- **Decomposition:** All numbers are made of other numbers and can be broken up into smaller parts:

  ? = 27 + 39

  "I can break apart 39 into 30 and 9.

  27 + 30 = 57

  57 + 9 = 66."

- **Compensation:** If one addend changes, the other addend can be adjusted to maintain the balance of the equation and make it easier to solve:

  ? = 27 + 39

  "39 is only 1 away from 40, so I can use 1 from 27 and add it to the 39 to make 40, and then I'm left with 26. 40 + 26 is easier to solve! 40 + 20 = 60, 60 + 6 = 66."

- **Constant difference:** The difference between two numbers does not change after you add or subtract the same quantity to both numbers:

  17 − 8 = ?

The distance from 8 to 17 is the same distance as 10 to 19. The distance is 9 numbers, so 17 − 8 = 9.

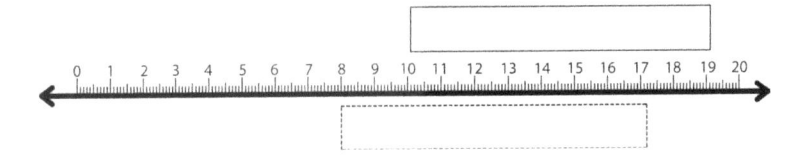

- **Commutative property:** Changing the order of two numbers in an addition problem does not change the result or the sum:

10 + 4 = 4 + 10

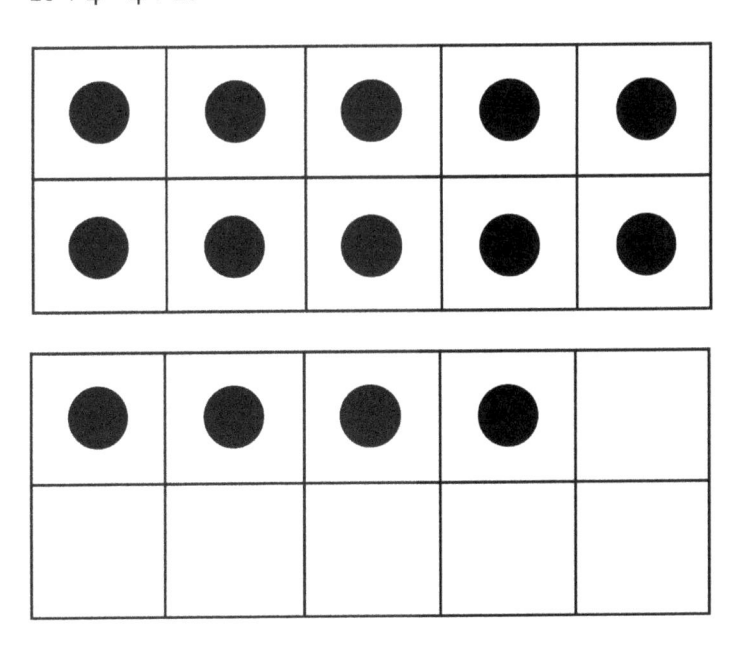

Integrating UDL in Teaching Additive Reasoning

Integrating UDL principles into the teaching and learning of additive reasoning represents a holistic approach that acknowledges and addresses the diversity of student learning needs. Providing multiple means of engagement ensures that students are motivated to learn about additive reasoning. Linking mathematical concepts to real-world scenarios relevant to students' lives not only piques their interest but also emphasizes the practical utility of what they're learning. Implementing games and collaborative activities incorporating additive reasoning, such as budgeting for a lemonade stand or cooking, can make learning enjoyable and applicable. Adapting your learning environment to support various forms of engagement is essential. This means designing physical and digital spaces that facilitate group work, individual study, and hands-on learning activities. Offering flexibility in timing, recognizing that students may need to work at different paces to master tasks, and being ready to provide additional support or enrichment are crucial for building purposeful learning experiences.

When teaching addition and subtraction, using a blend of visual aids, manipulatives, digital tools, and stories can illuminate the underlying relationships between numbers, moving beyond mere memorization to foster deeper comprehension. Concrete tools like tens frames and number lines, as we shared in the previous section, anchor abstract mathematical ideas in concrete visuals, aiding learners in comprehending these processes. Simultaneously, students need the opportunity to explore visual representations by representing those concrete tools with pencil and paper. They need their teacher to guide conversations to connect these models and scaffold their understanding of a more abstract representation with numbers and operations.

Providing students with various ways to express what they've learned is equally important. This could range from solving problems with tangible manipulatives and sketching out their thought processes to employing digital applications. Having students articulate their reasoning in multiple formats—whether written, oral, digital, or a combination thereof—can give you insight into their understanding of mathematical principles, which allows you to differentiate feedback and instruction as necessary. Providing continuous, constructive feedback and opportunities for student reflection is integral to a UDL-aligned approach. As students navigate additive reasoning tasks, encourage them to reflect on their experiences, the strategies they found beneficial, and any obstacles they faced to cultivate self-awareness and a growth mindset.

Blended Learning Highlight: Station Rotation

Station rotation is a strategy within the blended learning framework in which the classroom is divided into various stations. Each station is dedicated to distinct aspects of additive reasoning, blending online learning and offline activities as well as direct teacher instruction to cater to diverse learner needs.

One station is designated for teacher-led instruction, where educators can deliver explicit guidance tailored to students' individual learning needs. Utilizing data from formative assessments, teachers create flexible groups of students and ensure instruction is differentiated to meet each group's unique requirements. This setting provides an ideal opportunity for engaging students in math discourse, allowing for in-depth discussions and personalized feedback in a small-group environment. It can also support student reflection.

As students rotate through the stations, they encounter a variety of learning experiences designed with the UDL principles in mind. One station, for example, could be equipped with concrete manipulatives such as tens frames and number lines, inviting students to model addition and subtraction problems. Another station could leverage the power of digital technology, offering educational software that simulates real-world scenarios (e.g., like shopping exercises where students add items to their cart and calculate the total cost), combining abstract math principles with practical application. What kid wouldn't love the idea of shopping for their favorite snacks?

There could also be a collaborative station that encourages peer interaction through problem-solving activities. Here, students might work together to plan a class party within a budget, applying their additive reasoning skills to add and subtract costs. We love it when students have the opportunity to reflect on their collaboration on a large whiteboard or other vertical surface.

In the station rotation model, students benefit from the personalized attention of teacher-led instruction, the interactivity of digital tools, and the hands-on experience of manipulatives and group work. Some educators may wonder how to create a schedule for station rotation, so we want to share an example. For a class scheduled from 10:00 a.m. to 10:55 a.m., the station rotation schedule can be organized as follows.

Time	Addition Adventurers	Sum Seekers	Plus Pioneers	Counting Crew
10:00–10:10	Goals and Instructions			
10:10–10:20	Teacher Station	Planning a Party Station	Manipulative Station	Digital Station
10:20–10:30	Digital Station	Teacher Station	Planning a Party Station	Manipulative Station
10:30–10:40	Manipulative Station	Digital Station	Teacher Station	Planning a Party Station
10:40–10:50	Planning a Party Station	Manipulative Station	Digital Station	Teacher Station
10:50–10:55	Reflection			

The first 10 minutes is devoted to sharing the session goals and explaining the station organization. Each of the four groups spends 10 minutes at each station, and the last 5 minutes is dedicated to reflecting on the session's learning outcomes. Students rotate through various stations, including direct instruction at the Teacher Station, where they can interact closely with the educator. They also engage with digital tools at the Digital Station, utilize hands-on manipulatives at the Manipulative Station, and apply their knowledge to real-world scenarios at the Planning a Party Station. This approach diversifies the educational experience to cater to different learning preferences and needs and provides multiple means of engagement, representation, and action and expression.

The reflection period at the end allows students to consolidate their learning, share insights, and discuss how the concepts they learned can be applied outside the classroom, which is critical for student engagement. This dynamic learning environment is instrumental in bridging the gap between theoretical understanding and practical application, setting a robust stage for the next crucial phase of mathematical education.

Building a Foundation for Problem-Solving

To develop operational fluency, students need regular opportunities to solve meaningful problems relevant to their real lives using their own strategies. Often, these strategies are illuminated through the use of physical models like tens frames or number lines. Students may engage in a launch or number sense routine at the beginning of the math lesson to compare and contrast their strategies for adding 2-digit numbers. They may share their strategy, compare it with others, identify next steps, or represent strategies using a visual model.

> 23 + 18 = ?
>
> *Jack told me he started by adding 8 + 3 = 11. What could he do next?*
>
> *Charlie told me he started by adding 20 + 10 = 30. What could he do next?*
>
> *Avery told me she started by using 2 from the 3 and changing the problem to 21 + 20 = ? What could she do next?*

Students benefit from spending time in math class considering a situation, visualizing it, building it with manipulatives, modeling or representing their strategy, and explaining their thinking. It is our responsibility as their teachers to help them make sense of their strategies and construct meaning, building on their own thinking. Through this instructional model, students experience themselves as mathematicians, as the keepers of knowledge, as the ones who hold the power of thinking in their classrooms (Van de Walle et al., 2014). Simultaneously, students practice critical thinking, reasoning, and justifying viable arguments—all key components of the Common Core Standards for Mathematical Practice.

Consider the following task:

Mathematical goal: Represent and solve problems involving addition and subtraction within 100.

Avery and Hadley are making friendship bracelets. Avery put 18 beads on her bracelet. Hadley put 25 beads on her bracelet. How many more beads should Avery add to her bracelet if she wants to have the same number of beads as Hadley?

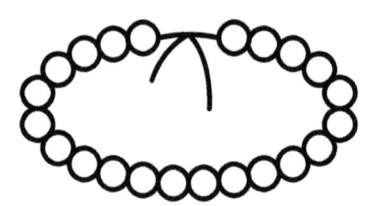

Let's start with what makes this a good task. First, it's relevant to a classroom with Maker Space Fridays, where beaded bracelets are a "go-to" station for many students. The teacher can readily re-create this situation on Fridays as a repeat of the mathematics discussed in this math class. This task has multiple entry points, as students can apply various strategies to find a solution, including reasoning strategies and accessing classroom manipulatives.

Unlock Access to Additive Reasoning

The teacher introduces this task in a way that removes barriers to accessing mathematics. They follow the All Learners Network's Problem Introduction Protocol (see https://www.alllearnersnetwork.com/blog/problem-intro-protocol). This begins with the teacher and students reading the problem together chorally and clarifying the meaning of words in the task. Students reflect on what the answer might look like as well as potential strategies for approaching the problem. The teacher ensures students have easy access to a variety of manipulatives that could be used to represent the situation, including actual beads from the Maker Space Station. As students work collaboratively to solve the task, the teacher walks around the room posing questions like, "I wonder if that will always work?" and "Can you show me how you solved that using a picture?" As the teacher moves about the classroom, they sort student strategies and sequence them to promote discussion and sense-making as students compare and contrast the models and strategies used by their peers (Smith & Stein, 2011). It is the teacher's role to facilitate this discussion as they pre-plan the order in which students will share and explain their problem-solving strategies. Student strategies may include the following:

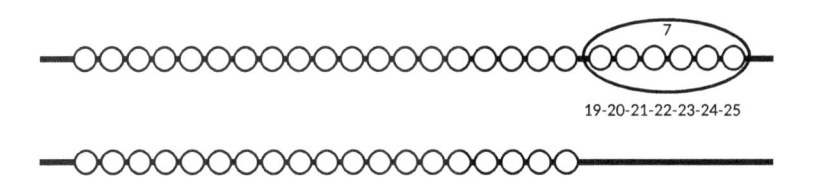

[Bead string diagram showing beads with a group of 7 circled on the right, labeled 19-20-21-22-23-24-25]

[Second bead string diagram]

As part of the class discussion, the teacher makes critical pedagogical decisions to highlight how these strategies are similar and different. When teachers ask students to share, compare, and justify their strategies, they strengthen the students' awareness of the goal and understanding of the content. Through this instructional model, students build the foundation for solving problems.

Simultaneously, they reflect on which strategy to use in a given situation, develop and enhance number skills and concepts, and build their own methods for computing fluently. Students make meaning of the math around them through these quality problem-solving opportunities.

Ms. Williams's Second Graders Explore Subtraction

Ms. Williams is a second-grade teacher in a school committed to the principles of UDL. Specifically, she's working toward providing more voice and choice throughout her students' day. In math class, Ms. Williams knows that having a relevant, real-life context is important for engaging her students in deep mathematical thinking. She also wants her students to be able to show their understanding using models and strategies that make sense to them. Recently, she polled her class to gather ideas based on their interests. Several students shared that they collect Pokemon trading cards, so Ms. Williams set up a math learning opportunity using the cards as the relevant context.

Ms. Williams: *Today, we are going to continue to practice our strategies for subtracting two-digit numbers. Let's take a look at this situation and talk about it!*

Ms. Williams shows a pile of Pokemon cards in front of the class. Suddenly, students are sitting up on their knees or crowding around the classroom carpet, trying to get a look at the cards Ms. Williams has just revealed in the front of the room.

Jack: *Whoa, Ms. Williams, is that a VMax? Where did you get that?!*

Marco: *Are we playing with those cards today, Ms. Williams?*

The class is visibly engaged in this topic before Ms. Williams has even entered the math task. She invites students to come closer to the pile of Pokemon cards. She even passes some of them around the room so students can feel them and talk to each other. She prompts students to discuss what they notice and wonder about the cards as they pass them around. After about five minutes, Ms. Williams asks students to return all the cards to the front of the room.

Ms. Williams: *What do you notice about this pile of Pokemon cards? What are you wondering about?*

Avery: *I noticed you have about 30 Pokemon cards there. That's not a huge collection. I'm wondering if you have more somewhere.*

Kyla: *I noticed there were 3 VMax cards in this pile. I'm wondering how many aren't VMax cards or if there's another type of card in that pile.*

Students continue noticing and wondering. As they share an idea, Ms. Williams writes it on the board next to the student's name. She knows it's important for students to feel heard and valued in the math classroom. She also knows that this is a way to build engagement in the task, give power back to the students as keepers of the information, and inspire future tasks students could solve after they solve her problem of the day.

Ms. Williams: *Thank you for sharing all of your ideas! I have one question that I've been thinking about that I'd love for us to solve together today. Avery was right; I have about 30 Pokemon cards. Specifically, I have 34 cards here today. But Mr. Jacobs (the second-grade teacher next door) told me that he has 67 Pokemon cards in his pile. How many more would I need to collect to have the same or more cards as Mr. Jacobs?*

Ms. Williams poses her question to the class and then writes it on the board. She rereads the question out loud and asks students the information they know from the problem. She also asks them to discuss what they need to find out.

Ms. Williams: *Okay, so we know we have 34 cards, and I want to have at least 67. We are trying to figure out how many more cards I need to have at least 67. What strategies could we use to solve this problem?*

Students turn and talk and brainstorm ideas. Some students use their whiteboards to write some ideas down, while others get up to grab some manipulatives from the manipulative shelf. Ms. Williams then prompts students to return to the carpet to share their strategies. As they do, Ms. Williams always responds, "Yes, you could try that." She knows students need to make their own choices when solving the math problem. She also notes students who may benefit from additional check-in during work time to ensure that their strategy makes sense for this situation.

Next, Ms. Williams has students work either independently or with a partner. The room is buzzing as some students use manipulatives, others write or sketch on whiteboards, and others draw in their math journals. When Ms. Williams notices a student sitting alone and not getting started, she walks over to them.

Ms. Williams: *Cam, I notice you haven't gotten started yet. What are you thinking about right now?*

Cam: *I'm not sure what to do.*

Ms. Williams: *Okay! I heard Mia share that she is using a number line starting at 34 and counting up to 67. I also heard Ben say that he is taking out 67 counters and then taking out the 34 I already have to see how many are left. Does one of those strategies sound interesting to you?*

Cam: *Yes, I like Ben's idea.*

Ms. Williams: *Awesome! Go sit with Ben and try to solve this problem together. I can't wait to see what you come up with.*

As students solve this problem, Ms. Williams walks around the room noting student strategies so she is prepared to facilitate the strategy-use discussion when the class regroups. In this scenario, Ms. Williams understood the mathematical goal and was able to pose a math task that both supported work toward that goal and was engaging for all students. She removed barriers to accessing the task by allowing students to consider the context, share strategies, and access tools independently. She allowed students choice not just in how they solved the problem, but in how they represented it, who they worked with, and where they worked in the classroom. It is clear that Ms. Williams considers *all* students in her classroom when designing learning opportunities.

* * *

Now that you have an example of the lesson, here's how Ms. Williams might structure this learning experience within the station rotation model:

- **Teacher station:** Ms. Williams can engage small groups with the subtraction problem she introduced, focusing on the difference in the number of Pokemon cards between her collection and that of Mr. Jacobs. This station allows for direct instruction tailored to each group's understanding, where she can introduce or reinforce strategies like using a number line or manipulatives to find the solution.

- **Digital station:** At this station, students might use tablets or computers to access digital math games that simulate Pokemon card collections. Through these games, they can practice subtracting two-digit numbers in various scenarios, such as trading cards with virtual partners or determining how many more cards they need to match or exceed a friend's collection.

- **Manipulative station:** This hands-on station could include actual or replica Pokemon cards and counters to help students physically manipulate objects to solve Ms. Williams's problem. Students can concretely see the subtraction process by grouping, adding, and removing cards or counters and develop their understanding of quantity and difference.

- **Planning a party station:** Building on the theme, this station could challenge students to plan a Pokemon card trade party. They would need to use subtraction to determine how many invitations to send out based on the number of students in the class versus the number of students they can host. They would also need to calculate how many snacks they need if some guests bring additional friends.

By the end of the math period, once students have participated in all stations, they could gather for a reflection session to share their strategies, discoveries, and how they applied their mathematical thinking to real-life contexts. Ms. Williams could facilitate this discussion, highlighting the variety of approaches taken and reinforcing the idea that there are many valid ways to understand and solve mathematical problems. This station rotation model, centered around student interests and grounded in UDL, exemplifies a learning environment where all students feel valued, engaged, and motivated to explore the world of mathematics.

REFLECTION QUESTIONS

1. How does the discussion of additive reasoning in this chapter align with your current practices and curriculum and how you design and deliver instruction on additive reasoning to students?

Unlock Access to Additive Reasoning

2. How can you give your students more voice and choice in how they learn and demonstrate their understanding of additive reasoning?
3. What concrete strategies can you immediately incorporate into your practice that align with evidence-based practices in UDL and blended learning, as discussed throughout this chapter?
4. How can you structure reflection periods in your lessons to help students consolidate their learning and recognize the application of math concepts outside the classroom?

6

Deepening Multiplication and Division Understanding

The Move From Memorization

One-size-fits-all instruction creates barriers that block the brilliance of many learners, especially students holding historically marginalized identities. For many of us, learning multiplication felt like a frenzy of memorization, timed tests, worksheets with rows of facts, and a lot of pressure. Consider how many adults you know who say they hate math or have a visceral reaction when recalling timed tests of basic facts. This style of instruction prioritizes one type of learning and in doing so excludes students who are not skillful memorizers (the vast majority of them), causing a great deal of harm to their perceptions of their capacity to learn math. It also sends the message that being able to memorize and compute quickly is more important than developing deep conceptual understanding.

Often, there is a perception that students who do not have their basic facts memorized through rote recall will struggle to learn more complex concepts. Students are then sorted into groups—those who are ready to take on more complicated tasks and those who are not—based solely on how quickly they can recite their facts. Rather than examining why memorization could be a barrier for some students, we effectively exclude students from deeper thinking opportunities when we prioritize rote memorization, perpetuating the unhelpful belief that some students can and some students can't do math (Bay-Williams & SanGiovanni, 2021). Instead, we must position all students as keepers of knowledge, power, and assets to our shared learning environment. In this chapter, we'll examine the challenges with timed tests and consider other strategies for building fluency through a deep conceptual understanding of multiplication and division.

Dangers of Timed Tests

Early number concepts are the foundation for reasoning and sense-making in more complex mathematics. Yet many school systems still use timed tests to predict future success. We cannot overstate how harmful timed tests are, and numerous research studies argue against them. One significant concern is the link between timed tests and the onset of math anxiety. Studies show that math anxiety can start as early as age 5, and this early anxiety tends to snowball, leading to further math difficulties and avoidance as children grow older. This anxiety affects a significant portion of the population, with about 50% of the US population experiencing it (Boaler, 2012).

To make matters worse, stressful math experiences like timed tests impede working memory, which is crucial for successfully executing cognitively demanding math problems. So not only do timed tests produce anxiety and impact working memory, but they are also an unreliable indicator of math fluency. For example, a student who can solve 6×9 using $(6 \times 5) + (6 \times 4)$ has a much deeper understanding of multiplication than a student who memorized $6 \times 9 = 54$. Opportunities to engage with multiplication and division should focus on sense-making and reasoning as the key components to demonstrating multiplication fluency—sending the message that all students can do math with the right tools, models, and strategies.

Building Fact Fluency Through Models

In *Young Mathematicians at Work: Constructing Multiplication and Division,* Catherine Twomey Fosnot and Maarten Dolk (2001) emphasize the importance of students constructing their own understanding of multiplication and division. Their models illuminate strategies focusing on key ideas like unitizing, number composition and decomposition, and application of the distributive property of multiplication. Through high-quality math tasks and relevant situations, students can generate and explore mathematical ideas to support their understanding of the concept.

Resonating with the core tenets of the UDL framework, Fosnot and Dolk (2001) explain that students learn along trajectories. As they move along these trajectories, students will develop a deep understanding of key mathematical concepts but not in the same sequence, at the same pace, or from the same entry point. To foster conceptual understanding, teachers must have a deep understanding of the trajectory of the mathematical concepts they are teaching—meaning they know the math they expect students to engage with and are prepared to build from students' differences in thinking and strategy use. In true UDL fashion, teachers need to provide a firm goal with flexible pathways to achieve that goal.

Fosnot and Dolk remind us, "It is not up to us, as teachers, to decide which pathways our students will use. Often, to our surprise, children will use a path we have not encountered before. That challenges us to understand the child's thinking" (p. 18). Students' ideas and interpretations of a situation vary in a single classroom. We are responsible for interpreting what a learner is doing and thinking and using this understanding to design the next instructional moves for that student. This is the only way to ensure we meet students where they are and move them forward. It also requires us to focus on what students can do and then build from their current understanding. To do this well, we need to recognize the variations in how a concept builds along a learning trajectory. For now, let's explore how multiplicative reasoning moves from counting objects by one to counting objects by group.

Big Ideas of Multiplication

In third and fourth grade, students are expanding on their understanding of place value and number composition and decomposition, and then applying this understanding to grouping models. Starting with unitizing, the central organizing idea in mathematics underpinning place value (i.e., ten objects are simultaneously 1 ten), students connect all they've discovered about our number system in preK through second grade. Students develop an understanding and application of the properties of numbers, specifically the distributive and associative properties. They can explore these concepts using visual models, including grouping models and arrays. Initially, students will count all objects by ones. Eventually, they may group smaller "chunks" within the larger group to find the total number of objects. Both strategies indicate strong additive reasoning to solve multiplication problems. Once we observe students moving toward organizing a multiplication situation into an array and using *both* dimensions—the length and the width—of the array to solve the multiplication problem, we know they've developed multiplicative reasoning (Fosnot & Dolk, 2001).

Consider the equation $4 \times 8 = ?$. At first, students will see this as 4 groups of 8 objects. They may make 4 piles or draw 4 circles with 8 items in each circle. They may count each object individually, skip count by 8, skip count in smaller chunks, or chunk smaller

Deepening Multiplication and Division Understanding

piles into larger piles to count. All of these strategies represent additive thinking in solving a multiplication problem. As learners move on, they begin to recognize that 4 groups represent one dimension, while 8 objects represent another dimension. Organized in an array, this would look like 4 rows and 8 columns. They may describe this as a "4 by 8 array." Now, students see the relationship between the two factors and can apply various strategies to solve it.

Through fourth grade, students build and expand on this reasoning as they explore multiplication and division with larger numbers. At this point, they can see that 27 × 18 represents a 27 by 18 rectangular area where 27 is the length and 18 is the width. They can apply their knowledge of place value to compose and decompose those factors and apply strategies to determine the total rectangular area or the product. Students need to build key skills and conceptual understandings through this trajectory. Each of these skills is demonstrated in the following section.

- **Unitizing:** A group of objects can be referred to as 1 unit. For example, each heart can be counted individually. There are 3 hearts in a group. Each of those groups is 1 group and there are 4 groups. Thus, 3 hearts are simultaneously 1 group. The parts together are now 1 new whole.

  We can also count each group of hearts as 1 group of 3. So, 1 group is also 3 hearts, and 4 groups of 3 is 12 hearts (4 × 3 = 12).

- **Composition and decomposition:** Composition means putting a number together using its parts. Decomposition means breaking down numbers into parts.

  I can see these five clouds as 2 clouds and 3 more, 1 cloud and 4 more, and so on.

  5 = 2 + 3
  5 = 1 + 4
  5 = 3 + 2
  5 = 4 + 1

  In multiplication, we use decomposition to support our use of the distributive property.

- **Distributive property:** Multiplying the sum of two or more addends by a number will give the same result as multiplying each addend individually by the number and then adding the products together.

  5 × 3 = (3 × 3) + (2 × 3)

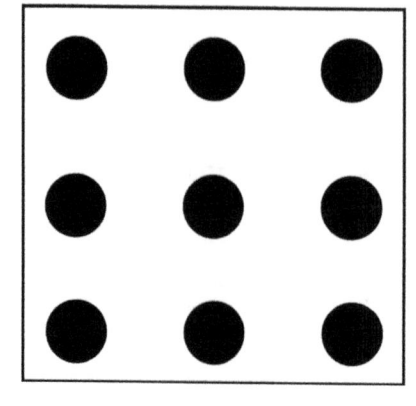

Deepening Multiplication and Division Understanding

- **Associative property:** When adding or multiplying more than two numbers, the result remains the same, irrespective of how they are grouped.

  $2 \times (7 \times 6) = (2 \times 7) \times 6$. $2 + (7 + 6) = (2 + 7) + 6$

  $35 \times 24 = ?$

  $24 \times 35 = ?$

  $20 \times 30 + 20 \times 5 + 4 \times 20 + 4 \times 5$

  $600 + 100 + 80 + 20 = 800$

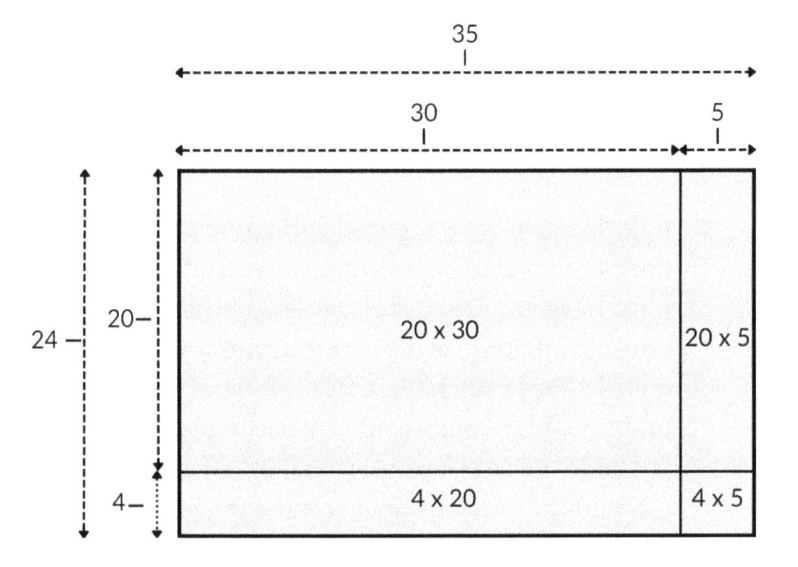

  [Area model diagram showing a 35 × 24 rectangle divided into four regions: 20 × 30, 20 × 5, 4 × 20, and 4 × 5.]

- **Commutative property:** Changing the order of the numbers being multiplied does not change the product. These both result in a total of 12 objects:

3 rows of 4   =   4 rows of 3

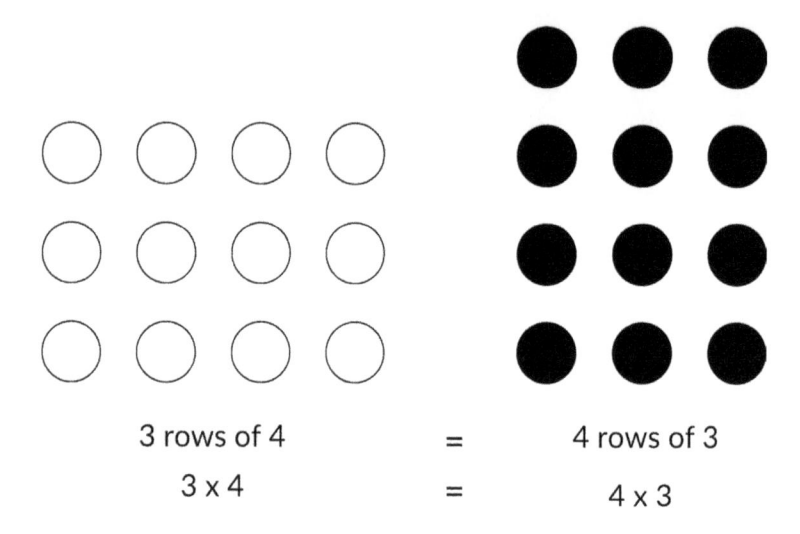

3 x 4   =   4 x 3

- **Relationship between multiplication and division:** Multiplication and division are inverse relationships. Students must have regular opportunities to explore this major relationship so they can derive strategies for solving that promote a deeper mathematical understanding. For example, in this task, students could choose to use partitive division to divide the total laps into smaller parts equally or could use multiplication by determining the missing factor:

  Christine is trying to complete a Fun Run as part of a schoolwide competition. She must run 48 laps around the middle school track in 6 days. If she wants to run the same number of laps each day, how many laps must she run each day to complete her goal?

- **Partitive and quotative division:** *Partitive division* refers to equal sharing or distributing where the total number of items and total number of groups are provided. The quotient is the number of items per group. *Quotative division* refers to grouping or repeated subtraction from the total.

Deepening Multiplication and Division Understanding

Quotative problems provide the total number of items to be divided and the number of items in each group. The quotient represents the number of groups.

- **Partitive:** There are 8 apples in a bag. The apples need to be shared equally between 2 bowls. How many apples will be in each bowl?
- **Quotative:** There are 8 apples in a bag. Cameron wants 4 apples in each basket. How many baskets will she need?

It's not important for students to know the names of these two types of division, but they must have experience with solving both problem types. What *is* important for students (and teachers) to recognize is that for any given division number sentence, two types of actions exist simultaneously and describe that same number sentence. For example, $8 \div 2 = 4$ can be considered as 8 grouped by 4s, so I have two groups, or as 8 shared between 2 bowls with 4 per bowl. This understanding promotes flexible thinking and the application of strategies that make sense to our students.

In summary, deepening students' understanding of multiplication and division requires moving beyond memorization and timed tests, which often create barriers and foster math anxiety. Instead, we must focus on building fluency through conceptual understanding and reasoning. By leveraging models and high-quality math tasks, we enable students to explore key mathematical concepts like unitizing, number composition and decomposition, and the properties of multiplication. Implementing a UDL approach means providing flexible pathways for all students to engage with and master these concepts. By recognizing the diverse ways students learn and think, and emphasizing the relationship between multiplication and division, we can support every learner in developing a robust mathematical foundation.

REFLECTION QUESTIONS

1. How does the shift from memorizing multiplication tables to building fluency through understanding numbers and patterns impact a student's long-term mathematical development? Discuss the potential benefits and challenges this shift might present in both the immediate classroom environment and in the student's future mathematical endeavors.

2. Considering the chapter's discussion on math anxiety, especially as it relates to timed tests, how might you redesign your assessment strategies to both evaluate students' understanding of multiplication and reduce anxiety? Propose alternative assessment methods that align with the principles of UDL and encourage a deeper understanding of multiplicative concepts.

3. How might teaching multiplication from a UDL approach help your students construct their multiplicative reasoning? What might be the implications for diverse learners in a classroom setting?

4. How can the concepts of multiplication, particularly the ideas of unitizing, composition, and decomposition, be applied to solve real-world problems? Propose a real-life scenario where these concepts could be effectively employed, and discuss the potential outcomes and learning opportunities that such an application would provide. Next, consider how you might structure the lesson with a blended learning playlist.

7

Inviting Students Into the World of Fractions

The Fraction Foundation

Throughout our writing journey, we were in constant communication, bouncing ideas and insights off each other. When drafting this chapter, we lovingly referred to it as wrangling "a beast" because we've worked with countless educators who have grappled with the challenge of teaching fractions.

Difficulty in teaching fractions stems not just from the concept itself but also from our own educational experiences with it and our need for increased understanding. By delving into the nitty-gritty of fractions—understanding them as numbers, grasping the part-to-whole concept, and getting familiar with unit and benchmark fractions—we can all get the training and tips we need to take on the challenge.

Proficiency with fractions is an important foundation for learning more advanced mathematics. Computation with all rational numbers is an essential milestone in algebra as students progress through middle school and into high school. However, many elementary teachers we interact with hold a deficit viewpoint of their own capability to fluently operate with fractions and support their students to do the same. For many of us, that's because of our own experiences learning fractions through elementary and middle school. The next time you walk through the airport or on the sidelines at a soccer game, stop and ask some folks what they remember about learning fractions. Most will respond with an algorithm "trick" like "keep, change, flip," but have no relevant context for why or when you keep, change, or flip anything. The rest will respond with a disgruntled "ugh" or "I don't remember anything at all."

This is to be expected when the majority of our instruction with fractions has involved rote memorization and application of a procedure. If you could memorize "keep, change, flip," you could divide a fraction by another fraction in an equation. You can search "dividing fractions" on the internet, and the results will include a slew of songs and mnemonic devices to memorize the procedure.

What happens when you are baking a cake and need a ½ cup of sugar but only have a ¼ cup scoop? How many of those ¼ cup scoops will you need to use? In other words, how many one-fourths are in one-half? What is ½ divided by ¼? Did you stop to pause and write out the "keep, change, flip" procedure? We're guessing not. How would you perceive your ability to operate with fractions if most of your experiences were grounded in relevant examples like this?

In the preceding example, we draw on the real-life experience of baking at home while building on what students already know about part to whole and decomposition, as described in previous chapters. In this chapter, we'll examine how to use our understanding of key mathematical concepts related to additive and multiplicative reasoning to build students' understanding of fractions.

Becoming Fluent in the Key Concepts of Fractions

There are some general elements of fractions and rational numbers that we are highlighting as critical for students to understand in order to develop strong fractional reasoning and the ability to operate with fractions in fifth and sixth grade. What we highlight, however, does not address everything you need to know about fractions.

First, it is important that we recognize and describe fractions as *numbers*. Often, we hear folks referring to a fraction like ⅓ as 1 part out of 3, unintentionally sending the message that the numerator and denominator are unrelated. This causes confusion for students because they're trying to apply their whole-number reasoning to a fraction that is, in fact, its own number or a single quantity. You can imagine what happens when we ask students to order and compare fractions in that scenario: "¼ is bigger than ½ because 4 is bigger than 2." Instead, we want students to use the relationship between the numerator and the denominator to visualize and describe a fraction: "½ is smaller than ¾ because ¾ is only a ¼ size piece from the whole and ½ is a ½ size piece from the whole." Students should be able to describe a fraction based on how many parts of that size are needed to make a whole. Fraction notation tells us the relationship between the part and the whole. Coming back to ⅓—our whole is broken up into 3 equal pieces, and we represent the value of one of those pieces as ⅓. The 1 is not disparate from the 3: 1 is a number, 3 is a number, ⅓ is its own number (Petit et al., 2022).

Equipartitioning

Understanding fractions requires an understanding of the concept of *equipartitioning*, or taking a whole and partitioning it into equal-sized portions or shares. The act of equipartitioning is a major component of generalizing fraction concepts. Using visual models, we can support students' understanding that fractional parts must be the same size but may not be the same shape. In addition, students develop the understanding that a fraction should always be interpreted in relation to the whole. This means

½ of a small pizza is not the same as ½ of a large pizza. The whole must be specified for them to be able to accurately compare and order fractions. Students subsequently begin to understand that when partitioning a whole into more equal shares, the parts become smaller (Van de Walle et al., 2014). As an example, consider the following problem:

> If I share a candy bar with three people, each of us gets ⅓ of the candy bar. But when my brother and his friend ask to share the candy bar, and we want to share that candy bar equally, we will each get ⅕ of the candy bar. That ⅕ piece is smaller than the ⅓ piece I originally would have had.

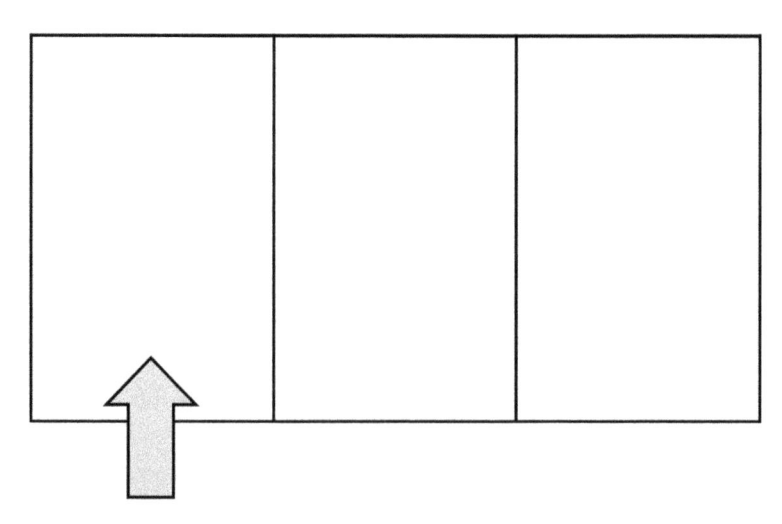

This piece is ⅓ of the whole rectangle.

Partitioning and Iterating

Another key component of fractional understanding is the ability to partition and iterate unit fractions. For example, we want students to understand that ⅔ is composed of a ⅓ and another ⅓ size piece, and we represent that total as the number ⅔. You may notice that the foundational understanding of composition and decomposition of numbers is again at play here. A preschooler's understanding that 5 is composed of 2 + 3, but also 4 + 1, but also 1 + 1 + 1 + 1 +1 is the same understanding we want our fourth and fifth graders to have when recognizing that ⅘ is composed of ⅖ + ⅖ or ⅗ + ⅕ or ⅕ + ⅕ + ⅕ + ⅕ + ⅕.

Equivalence

Finally, we need students to understand that when fractions are equivalent, they represent the same-sized piece from the same-sized whole but using different fractional parts. Estimating, comparing, and ordering fractions based on reasoning is critical for sense-making through visual models like fraction bars and number lines. This is imperative as students navigate the difference between rational and whole numbers (Van de Walle et al., 2014).

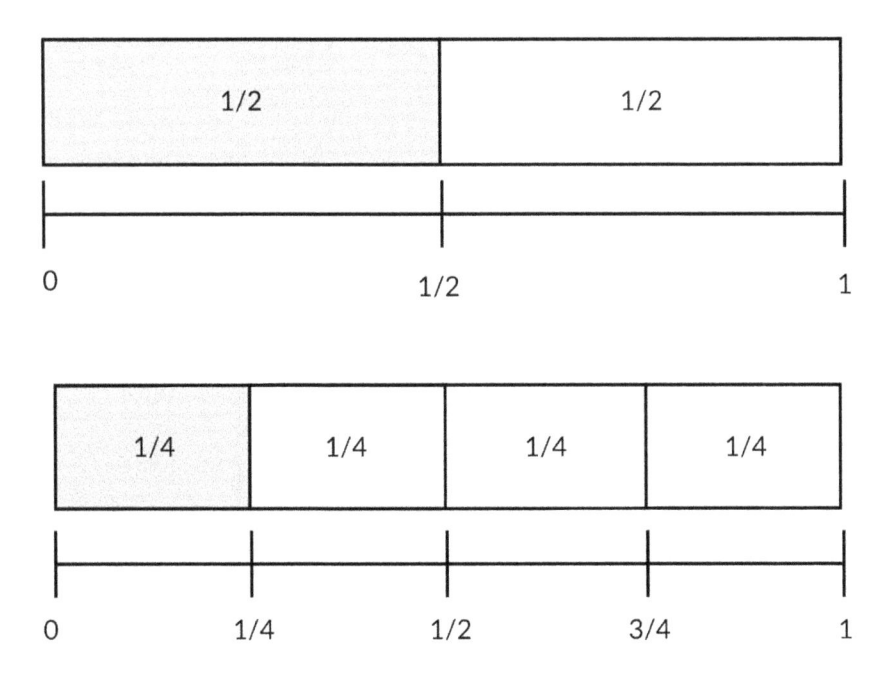

1/2	1/2

```
0              1/2              1
|---------------|---------------|
```

1/4	1/4	1/4	1/4

```
0       1/4      1/2      3/4      1
|--------|--------|--------|--------|
```

Universal Design for Learning in Mathematics Instruction (K-5)

Students also need opportunities to work with various representations of fractions, including set and region models.

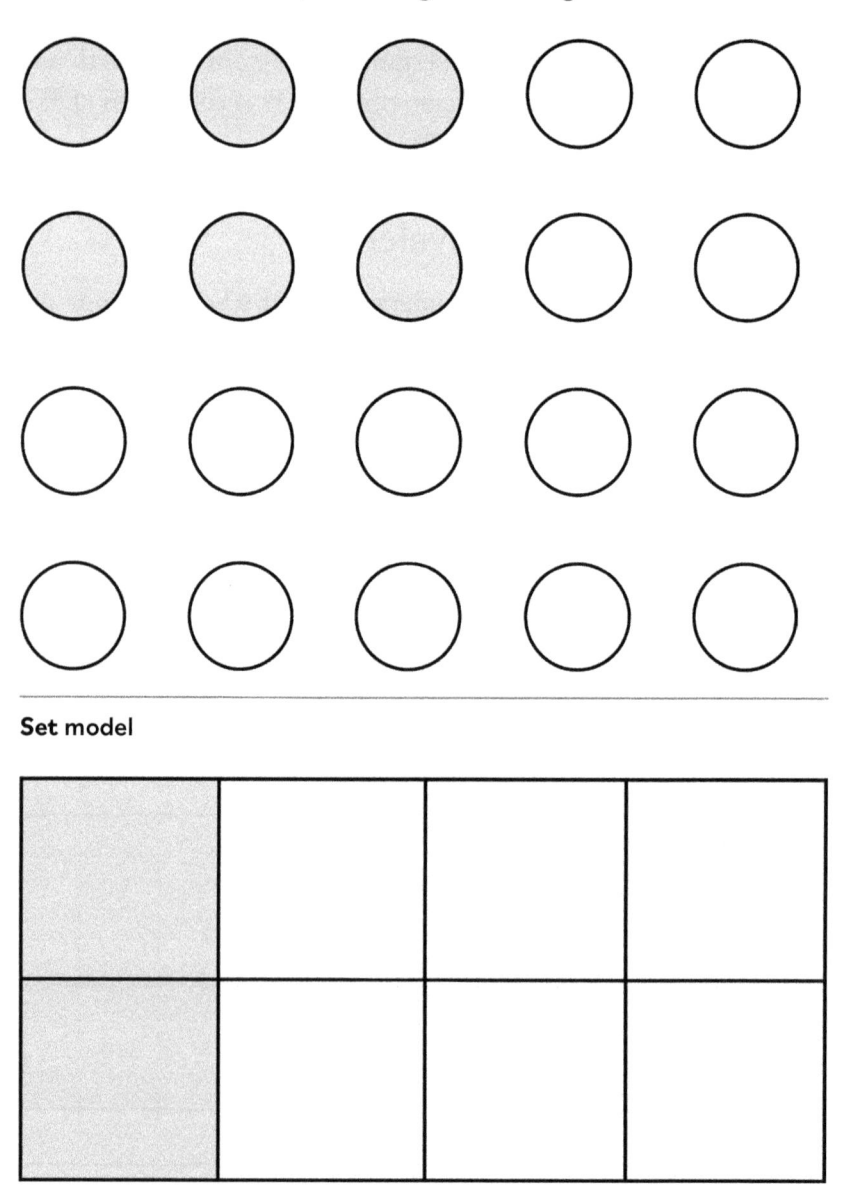

Set model

Region model

These models help students make sense of fractions conceptually. Learners need to develop a concrete realization of a fraction to form a mental picture of what one looks like. As students move through elementary and middle school, we often see teachers pulling away from concrete and visual models far too quickly. Our fourth-, fifth-, and sixth-grade students need to spend just as much time building with concrete models like fraction bars and drawing representations of fractions like fraction strips and number lines as our kindergarten, first, and second-grade students do building numbers using tens frames and drawing representations like base-10 pieces and number lines.

Ordering and Sequencing

As students develop a sense of fractions, they also benefit from being able to explore ordering and sequencing fractions as well as comparing fractions. When students are asked to use reasoning to order a set of fractions from least to greatest and then compare those numbers to a half or a whole, they bolster their understanding of fractions as numbers. Students need opportunities to compare numerators, compare denominators, and compare fractions to benchmark fractions like ½ and 1. This gives them the background they need to find common denominators, create equivalent fractions, and add and subtract fractions.

A fraction, like any number, is a single point on a number line that does not end. It is critical that all students can make sense of this. When we imagine 53, we want to imagine all of the numbers that came before 53 and those that come after 53. We practice this when we ask students to count on and count back. Students use their understanding of the number 53 to consider the number that would come next in the counting sequence. We need students to apply this understanding when visualizing fractions. The fraction ⅔ is a number, and we can consider the fractions that came before ⅔ and the fractions that come after ⅔. We can even count by thirds!

Moreover, we need students to recognize that each fraction with a numerator greater than 1 is composed of unit fractions. Just like any number greater than 1 comprises unit whole numbers, each fraction comprises unit fractions. We can think of 53 as 53 units of 1 or even as 5 units of 10 and 3 more. I can think of ⅔ as two ⅓s or ⅓ + ⅓. Students need to understand unit fractions as the building block of all fractions by applying their understanding of equipartitioning, composition, and decomposition. In the same way, they need to extend this understanding of one whole as the building block of all whole numbers (Petit et al., 2022).

Baking With Mrs. E

Mrs. E is a math interventionist working with a small group of fifth-grade students to support their understanding of fractions. Simultaneously, this particular group of students is working to build their positive mindsets when it comes to mathematics. Mrs. E knows that by the time students get to fifth grade, they have many instilled unhelpful beliefs about their perceived math abilities. She regularly hears these students say, "I'm so dumb" or "I'm bad at math, so I have to come here."

To start their work together, Mrs. E asked students to reflect on their thoughts and feelings about math. She asked each student to write, draw, or record their "math story," ensuring that students had some voice and choice in how they represented their thoughts and feelings. At the close of this project, Mrs. E learned a lot about the types of experiences these students had in math as early as 10 and 11 years old. Students described zoning out, sitting in the back of the room, refusing to raise their hands or share ideas, feeling "dumb," and believing they had nothing to contribute in math class. Some explained that their parents hated math, so they do too. Mrs. E knew she needed to shift these students' mindsets and experiences around math and ensure they could experience the joy of doing math.

Mrs. E: *I loved learning about your math stories. It really helped me understand you better and helped me think about ways that I can support your math learning. I know all of you can do math, and I want to help you see why I know that.*

Students: *Ughhh, this is going to be so boring.*

Mrs. E: *[Plunging forward like the emboldened, intentional teacher she is] We are going to bake some cookies today. I asked Mr. Jenkins if it was okay to use the kitchen this afternoon and he said yes! I also asked Ms. Webb and Mr. Robinson if you could stay a little longer today, and they agreed!*

Students: *Can we eat the cookies after?*

Mrs. E: *Of course! That's the best part!*

Mrs. E had already set out the ingredients and baking tools in the kitchen. She provided each student with a copy of the recipe and ensured it was available digitally so everyone could follow along. She intentionally left a ¼ cup and ½ cup scoop on the table, excluding the other scoops from the supplies. As students entered the kitchen, they reviewed some safety expectations and then got to work dissecting the recipe.

Mrs. E: *The first ingredient is 2½ cups of white flour. How can we ensure we get exactly 2½ cups of flour in this large mixing bowl? [Now, in the spirit of UDL, we have to ensure that Mrs. E also has gluten-free flour so students can choose what's best for their cookies!!]*

Sammi: *We need to use those measuring scoops to scoop it out of the bag and put it in the bowl.*

Mrs. E: *Excellent! Go ahead and do that for us, Sammi.*

Sammi: *Okay, I can do the ½ cups with this half-cup scoop. Then I need to do the whole cups. So I need two of the half scoops to make one cup of flour, and then I'll do that again to get another cup of flour.*

Josephine: *Wait, so that means you just need to do 5 scoops with that scoop—you can just count 1, 2, 3, 4, 5, and that will be 5 half cups. That's the same as 2½ cups of flour.*

Mrs. E: *Interesting! Any other ideas?*

Milo: *Sammi could use that ¼ scoop—it would be a lot more scoops. She'd need four of those for each cup of flour. So she'd need like 10 scoops.*

Sammi: *Wait! That's cool. We need 5 of the half-cup scoops and 10 of the quarter-cup scoops.*

Josephine: *Yeah, that's because you need two of the ¼ scoops to get one of the ½ scoops, so for every one scoop of ½, you need two scoops of ¼.*

Milo: *So you need double the scoops.*

Mrs. E: *I wonder why?*

Sammi: *WAIT. That's because ¼ is half of ½, so you'd need DOUBLE the scoops!*

Mrs. E: *That's so interesting! Okay, let's continue with this recipe. This is making me want to enjoy these cookies!*

Mrs. E continued this lesson with her students, jotting down some interesting findings they made as they navigated a recipe with only the two sizes of scoops. When they got back to class, she shared their thoughts and facilitated a discussion about halving and doubling and how that related to the work they did today.

Milo: *Wait, Mrs. E—so this is why when you divide ½ by ¼ you get 2. Because you need two ¼s to make a ½.*

Mrs. E: *Wow! That is so interesting! Let's keep exploring that.*

Mrs. E created a learning opportunity for her students that allowed them to experience math in real life. They got to explore fractions in a nonthreatening environment and were allowed the opportunity to construct their understanding. Now, Mrs. E has an engaging, relevant context to return to and build on students' understanding. She also provided a learning opportunity that allowed students to see themselves as mathematicians, using real math in real life. This one scenario will not drastically impact her students' perceptions of their own abilities in math, but we know that these small moments build on each other, slowly shifting her students' mindsets.

* * *

Mrs. E's baking lesson demonstrates the power and promise of UDL. Now, we know you don't all have kitchens ready and waiting for a math lesson, but there are school cafeterias, so it's worth asking! Whether you're baking cookies or using a recipe to make slime, there is value in building math engagement.

By launching the lesson with an invitation for students to share their "math stories" in a format of their choice, Mrs. E not only acknowledged the importance of students' emotions and beliefs about math but also actively worked to build a positive learning environment that helped to create relevance and optimize motivation. This is a critical foundation for deep engagement. The real-life application of baking cookies served not just as a fun activity but as a meaningful context for learning, demonstrating the relevance and joy of math in everyday life. (After all, who doesn't love cookies?)

To provide multiple means of representation, Mrs. E integrated visual and digital resources, along with concrete manipulatives, to ensure all students could access the content and build understanding. Providing the recipe in both photocopy and digital formats allowed for flexibility in how students followed along. For example, multilingual learners could translate the recipe and read or listen first in L1 (their first language or the primary language they learned at home). The strategic use of only two sizes of measuring scoops challenged students to engage with fractions in a tangible way, promoting a deeper conceptual understanding through the physical manipulation of materials. The collaborative aspect of the lesson, where students were encouraged to discuss and explore various strategies for measuring ingredients, ensured that multiple representations of mathematical concepts were explored, enriching students' understanding through peer interaction.

Mrs. E also designed her lesson with multiple means of engagement by embedding numerous opportunities for students to share problem-solving strategies in reflective discussions. This reflective discussion, both during and after the baking activity, ensured that students had a platform to express their understanding in their own words, reinforcing their learning and allowing Mrs. E to assess their comprehension in a natural and engaging way. Using this activity as a formative assessment and encouraging student self-reflection can help Mrs. E decide on the most appropriate instructional strategies as the class continues their exploration of fractions.

This chapter only scratches the surface of the critical understandings related to fractions. Many of our experiences in elementary school and our preservice teaching opportunities did not prepare us to deeply understand fractions so that we can readily compute them fluently and flexibly. Our learning of fractions often involved the "do it like me" approach, producing a very surface-level understanding of the concept that has left many educators and students with gaps in their fraction knowledge. For additional support and a deeper exploration of fractions, consider exploring *A Focus on Fractions: Bringing Research to the Classroom*, 3rd Edition (Petit et al., 2022). This resource offers valuable insights and practical strategies to enhance your understanding and teaching of fractions.

REFLECTION QUESTIONS

1. Considering the chapter's emphasis on building a deep understanding of fractions, what strategies can you and your colleagues employ to help students (and perhaps yourselves!) unlearn misconceptions about fractions that stem from rote memorization?

2. How can you create more lessons like Mrs. E's baking activity that connect fractions to real-world experiences? Reflect on the importance of these connections in helping students see the relevance of fractions in their daily lives and in building a positive math identity.

3. Reflect on how the principles of UDL were incorporated into Mrs. E's lesson on fractions. How can you apply these principles more broadly in your own math instruction to support diverse learners and encourage a deeper understanding of mathematical concepts?

Conclusion

Learning Takes Vulnerability

We cannot close out this book without addressing the vulnerability it takes for teachers and students to examine their beliefs about themselves and their competence in math. In her book *Daring Greatly*, Brené Brown describes vulnerability as "uncertainty, risk, and emotional exposure" (Brown, 2012). When we get that shaky, upset stomach, unstable, out-of-our-comfort-zone feeling, we have to push through that discomfort to take a risk. That is the sweet spot, the learning spot—the growth spot. Neuroscientists often call this moment the "aha" moment, or the rush of excitement at a moment of insight.

In a recent All Hands Meeting at the All Learners Network—intended for participants to share company-wide information, exchange ideas, take risks, and collaborate—CEO and founder Dr. John Tapper presented the team with a "low-floor, high-ceiling" high school–level math task. He asked everyone in the company to engage in the math exercise by providing some context, asking probing questions to allow entry points for all, and encouraging the team to work collaboratively on vertical whiteboards. As diligent students, everyone jumped into the task in teams, starting from their own places of readiness and sharing ideas with others. John's facilitation allowed the company—sales, marketing, operations, facilitators, and administrators—to dive into a complex, rigorous math task. It was accessible and engaging but not instantly solvable. It required some productive struggle, resulting in several lightbulb or aha moments for participants. Then, the team had the chance to reflect, discuss, and process the experience.

At the end of the debrief, one team member raised her hand and shared, "I have a master's degree in teaching mathematics, have 20 years of teaching experience, and do this work every single day, and still, the moment you told us we could get to work, I panicked at first." A quick glance around the room showed slow nods and wide eyes in recognition. Another colleague chimed in, "Same! I felt the exact same way." Yet another colleague shared, "Thank you for saying that; I was worried I was the only one."

This was a room full of educators, math specialists, and experts—yet those deeply ingrained, unhelpful beliefs about competence in mathematics showed up. The shame of not knowing, not being good enough, or fear of being wrong still existed in a room of so-called math people.

Math and Happiness

The thought of student engagement often brings joy and happiness, but as we lean into productive struggle, we'll likely experience confusion, cognitive dissonance, or, let's face it, some frustration. Not every moment of learning creates happiness in the short term, but goodness, those aha moments feel good! True happiness is more than the jolt of recognizing that you can accomplish something you thought was out of your reach. Because we want students to experience short-term accomplishments and long-term success, it's important to discuss the different types of happiness, as the distinction is important.

When people think about happiness, they often think about hedonic happiness, or seeking pleasure and having fun. Certainly, we want this for our learners. Both of us enjoy going out with

Conclusion

friends, having a great cocktail, or snuggling with puppies. We are also both hoping to snag tickets to a Noah Kahan concert—hedonism at its finest!! All of these things bring us pleasure and make us feel good. That is very different from another type of happiness called *eudaimonic* happiness.

Eudaimonic happiness is about fulfilling our purpose. In research, it has been referred to as happiness plus meaningfulness (Ryan & Deci, 2001). It's about setting personalized goals and carving out the paths to accomplish something great. As much as we love snuggling puppies and would love to have a coffee with Noah Kahan, it doesn't compare to our work dismantling inaccessible education systems or the joy and pride we feel in raising our beautiful families.

Deep engagement in mathematics transcends the immediate satisfaction of solving a problem or collaborating within a learner community. It involves equipping students with the essential skills to set ambitious goals, maintain long-term commitment to their objectives, and possess the problem-solving capabilities and motivation required to achieve their dreams.

When we universally design mathematics education, we acknowledge and strive to dismantle the barriers created by one-size-fits-all instruction and the superficiality of shallow learning. To do this well, we have to have high expectations, presume competence, and continue to strengthen a deep belief in our students' potential and our own ability as educators. By fostering environments that champion the deep understanding of mathematics alongside the development of essential problem-solving skills, we're not just teaching numbers or equations, we're empowering students to construct meaningful narratives around their learning that resonate with their aspirations and fuel their journey toward achieving them.

In essence, we're committed to transforming the traditional educational landscape into learning environments where students can flourish academically and thrive in their personal journeys for eudaimonic happiness. Sometimes, when we work with educators, they share that shifting their instructional practices is difficult. We don't want to minimize the challenge of this change. Change is hard! We do, however, want to highlight that this is the work we are called to do. Ultimately, when we work through these challenges together, we can also experience eudaimonic happiness.

Throughout this book, we've challenged you to consider your perceptions of students' capacity to learn math well, as well as your own capacity to learn and teach math well. By now, we expect you to recognize the impact of math learning experiences on your own math identity. When we consider our historically resilient students' perspectives on their perceived capabilities in mathematics, we must examine our instructional practices to ensure that our student-to-teacher relationships affirm mathematics identities and support students' positive learning experiences in math class.

As described throughout this book, our goal in our math classrooms is to provide opportunities to build curiosity and wonder and denounce the over-proceduralized, "do it like me" style of teaching we often see in elementary math classrooms. Ultimately, the goal is to transform our classrooms into ecosystems where diverse learning paths coexist harmoniously, and each student's relationship with mathematics is strengthened.

Final Thoughts

The journey to deepen understanding in mathematics requires a collective effort to shift from rote memorization to fostering conceptual understanding. By embracing vulnerability and recognizing the value of productive struggle, we create learning environments that promote immediate engagement and long-term success. The integration of UDL principles ensures that all students, regardless of their background or learning style, have

Conclusion

access to meaningful and challenging math education. As we continue to refine our practices and support one another in this endeavor, we pave the way for a future where every student can experience the joy and fulfillment of mathematical discovery.

REFLECTION QUESTIONS

1. Consider a time when you felt vulnerable in your own learning, particularly in mathematics. What emotions and challenges did you experience, and how did pushing through that discomfort contribute to your learning? Discuss how this personal experience influences your teaching practices regarding encouraging vulnerability among your students.

2. Productive struggle is key to deep learning but can be uncomfortable for students and teachers. Reflect on an instance from your teaching or learning where experiencing this struggle led to significant insight or aha moments. How can you incorporate productive struggle in your classroom to enhance students' mathematical understanding while managing their emotional responses effectively?

3. Discuss the differences between hedonic and eudaimonic happiness in the context of learning mathematics. How can understanding these forms of happiness influence your approach to teaching math? Share methods to balance immediate, joyous engagement with the long-term, meaningful pursuit of mathematical competence in *all* your students.

References

Aguirre, J. M., Mayfield-Ingram, K., & Martin, D. B. (2013). *The impact of identity in K–8 mathematics: Rethinking equity-based practices.* National Council of Teachers of Mathematics.

Anyon, J. (1980). Social class and the hidden curriculum of work. *The Journal of Education, 162*(1), 67–92.

Bay-Williams, J. M., & SanGiovanni J. J. (2021). *Figuring out fluency in mathematics teaching and learning, grades K–8: Moving beyond basic facts and memorization (Corwin Mathematics Series)* (1st ed.). Corwin Press.

Biklen, D., & Burke, J. (2006). Presuming competence. *Equity & Excellence in Education, 39*(2), 166–175.

Boaler, J. (2012). Timed tests and the development of math anxiety (opinion). *Education Week.* https://www.edweek.org/teaching-learning/opinion-timed-tests-and-the-development-of-math-anxiety/2012/07

Brown, B. (2012). *Daring greatly: How the courage to be vulnerable transforms the way we live, love, parent, and lead.* Gotham.

CASEL. (2024). *SEL 3 signature practices.* https://signaturepractices.casel.org/

Chardin, M., & Novak, K. (2020). *Equity by design: Delivering on the power and promise of UDL.* Corwin Press.

Ching, B. H., & Nunes, T. (2017). The importance of additive reasoning in children's mathematical achievement: A longitudinal study. *Journal of Educational Psychology, 109,* 477–508.

Claessens, A., Duncan, G. J., & Engel, M. (2009). Kindergarten skills and fifth-grade achievement: Evidence from the ECLS-K. *Economics of Education Review, 28*(4), 415–427.

Clements, D. H., & Sarama, J. (2014). *Learning and teaching early math* (2nd ed.). Routledge.

Cobb, F., & Krownapple, J. (2019). *Belonging through a culture of dignity: The keys to successful equity implementation.* Mimi and Todd Press.

Delpit, L. D. (2012). *"Multiplication is for White people": Raising expectations for other people's children.* The New Press.

Donnellan, A. M. (1984). The criterion of the least dangerous assumption. *Behavioral Disorders, 9(2),* 141–150.

Dweck, C. S. (2008). *Mindset: The new psychology of success* (paperback ed.). Ballantine Books.

Dysarz, K. (2018). *Checking in: Are math assignments measuring up?* The Equity Trust. https://hsredesign.org/wp-content/uploads/2019/02/CheckingIn_MATH-ANALYSIS_FINAL_5.pdf

EdReports. (2024). *Selecting for quality: 6 key adoption steps.* https://www.edreports.org/resources/adoption-steps

Fabina, J., Hernandez, E. L., & McElrath, K. (2023). *School enrollment in the United States: 2021* (American Community Survey Reports). U.S. Census Bureau.

Five Moore Minutes. (2021, February 1). *The importance of presuming competence* [Video]. YouTube. https://www.youtube.com/watch?v=6Mq8sQTEhG8

Fosnot, C. T., & Dolk, M. (2001, February 1). *Young mathematicians at work: Constructing multiplication and division.* Heinemann.

Goffney, I., Gutiérrez, R., & Boston, M. (Eds.). (2018). Rehumanizing mathematics for Black, Indigenous, and Latinx students. *Annual Perspectives in Mathematics Education, vol. 2018.* National Council of Teachers of Mathematics.

Gutiérrez, R. (2012). Context matters: How should we conceptualize equity in mathematics education? In B. Herbel-Eisenmann, J. Choppin, D. Wagner, & D. Pimm (Eds.), *Equity in discourse for mathematics education* (pp. 17–33). Springer.

Hammond, Z. (2014). *Culturally responsive teaching and the brain: Promoting authentic engagement and rigor among culturally and linguistically diverse students.* Corwin Press.

Hattie, J. (2012). *Visible learning for teachers: Maximizing impact on learning.* Routledge/Taylor & Francis Group.

References

Huinker, D. (2020). *Catalyzing change in early childhood and elementary mathematics: Initiating critical conversations.* National Council of Teachers of Mathematics.

Jitendra, A. K., Harwell, M. R., Dupuis, D. N., & Karl, S. R. (2013). Effects of a research-based intervention to improve seventh-grade students' proportional problem solving: A randomized experiment. *Journal of Research on Educational Effectiveness, 6*(4), 331–357.

Lang, J. M. (2016). Small changes in teaching: The first 5 minutes of class. *The Chronicle of Higher Education.* https://www.chronicle.com/article/small-changes-in-teaching-the-first-5-minutes-of-class/

Liljedahl, P. (2020). *Building thinking classrooms in mathematics grades K–12.* Corwin Press.

Marlow, A., & Novak, K. (2022). *Making math accessible for all students.* Edutopia. https://www.edutopia.org/article/making-math-accessible-all-students/

McCardle, T. (2020). A critical historical examination of tracking as a method for maintaining racial segregation. *Educational Considerations, 45*(2).

National Center for Science and Engineering Statistics (NCSES). (2023). *Diversity and STEM: Women, minorities, and persons with disabilities.* Directorate for Social, Behavioral and Economic Sciences, National Science Foundation. https://ncses.nsf.gov/pubs/nsf23315/

National Governors Association Center for Best Practices, Council of Chief State School Officers. (2010). *Common Core State Standards (Math and Standards of Mathematical Practice), Grades K–12.* National Governors Association Center for Best Practices, Council of Chief State School Officers.

National Teacher and Principal Survey (NTPS). (2017–2018). National Center for Education Statistics, US Department of Education.

Nation's Report Card. (2022). *Largest score declines in NAEP mathematics at grades 4 and 8 since initial assessments in 1990.* National Assessment of Educational Progress. https://www.nationsreportcard.gov/highlights/mathematics/2022/

Novak, K. (2022). *UDL now!: A teacher's guide to applying Universal Design for Learning* (3rd ed.). CAST, Inc.

Oyserman, D., Brickman, D., Bybee, D., & Celious, A. (2006). *Fitting in matters: Markers of in-group belonging and academic outcomes.*

Institute for Social Research, The University of Michigan, Association for Psychological Science.

Petit, M., Laird, R., Ebby, C., & Marsden, E. (2022). *A focus on fractions: Bringing research to the classroom.* Routledge.

Ryan, R. M., & Deci, E. L. (2001). On happiness and human potentials: A review of research on hedonic and eudaimonic well-being. *Annual Review of Psychology, 52*(1), 141–166.

Schwartz, S. (2023). *Are schools choosing high-quality math curricula? A new database offers clues.* Education Week. https://www.edweek.org/teaching-learning/are-schools-choosing-high-quality-math-curricula-a-new-database-offers-clues/2023/10

Secada, W., Medina, E., & Avalos, M. (2017). A framework for modifying mathematics tasks for accessibility. *Teaching for Excellence and Equity in Mathematics, 8*(1), 23–30.

Smith, M., & Stein, M. (2011). *5 practices for orchestrating productive struggle in mathematics discussions.* National Council of Teachers of Mathematics.

Stein, M., Smith, M., Henningsen, M., & Silver, E. (2000). *Implementing standards-based mathematics instruction: A casebook for professional development.* Teachers College of New York.

Tan, P., Padilla, A., Mason, E., & Sheldon, J. (2020). *Humanizing disability in mathematics education: Forging new paths.* Resource Guide, National Council of Teachers of Mathematics, Inc.

Tapper, J. (2012). *Solving for why: Understanding, assessing, and teaching students who struggle with math, grades K–8.* Math Solutions.

Tucker, C. (2023, January 20). *The art of self-pacing: How to build playlists that keep students on track.* Dr. Catlin Tucker. https://catlintucker.com/2023/01/self-pacing-playlists/

Van de Walle, J. A., Lovin, L. H., Karp, K. S., & Bay-Williams, J. M. (2014). *Teaching student-centered mathematics: Developmentally appropriate instruction for grades pre-K–2.* Pearson.

Vermont Agency of Education. (2024). *Act 173.* https://education.vermont.gov/vermont-schools/education-laws/act-173

Wolpert, S. (2018). *Why so many U.S. students aren't learning math.* UCLA Newsroom. https://newsroom.ucla.edu/stories/why-so-many-u-s-students-arent-learning-math

Index

A
abilities, perceived, 37, 40, 46, 50
abstract concepts, 15–16, 71
access to education
    equity in, 2, 3
    via high-quality materials, 25–26
    and student choice, 20–22, 83
    and teacher beliefs/skills, 40–44
    teacher/student identity and, 10–11
achievement gap, 13
action and expression
    by all students, 51
    multiple means of, 17–19, 69, 74
active learning, 24
additive reasoning, 57, 67–85, 90–91
"aha" moments, 111, 112
algebra, 3–4, 69, 97
Algebra Project, 2, 4
All Learners Network, 43, 44, 79, 111
anxiety, 88, 112
Anyon, Jean, 51
arithmetic
    additive reasoning, 67–85
    early numeracy skills, 55–66
    multiplication/division, 87–96
    subtraction, 29, 68–84, 94, 103
assessment
    multiple means of, 17–19
    self-assessments, 35
    timed tests, 20, 74, 88

associative property, 90, 93
assumptions. *See* beliefs/assumptions
auditory representations, 16

B
beliefs/assumptions
    least dangerous assumption, 50
    and presumed competence, 49–50
    of students, 44, 46
    of teachers, 41, 42–45, 51, 114
    vulnerability of facing, 111
belonging, sense of, 26, 36, 45
Belonging Through a Culture of Dignity (Cobb and Krownapple), 36
blended learning, 33–35
Brown, Brené, 111

C
calculus, 69
cardinality, 59
challenges, tackling
    of executive function, 18
    of fractions, 97
    via meaningful tasks, 27
    multiple representations and, 17
    via partner playlists, 34
    as productive struggle, 60, 111–112
    rewards following, 114
    student agency and, 50
    and teacher assumptions, 51–52

choice
- in early counting tasks, 62–65
- and "firm goals, flexible means," 14
- in solving/presenting solutions, 83, 89
- voice and, 12

civil rights, 2, 4

classroom work
- in-class relationships and, 46
- collaborative learning in, 114
- for early learners, 61
- as a group, 9
- rigor in, 2
- and sharing solutions, 65
- start-time activities, 47–48

coaches, beliefs of, 44

cognitive demand, high, 30–33

coherent materials, 25

collaborative learning, 14–15, 33, 35, 65, 74, 76

college
- algebra as prerequisite for, 3
- inequity in access to, 11
- minimal requirements for, 7–8

Common Core State Standards, 24, 78

communication, effective, 13

commutative property, 73, 93

compensation, equation balance and, 72

competence, student, 18, 26, 49–52

composition of numbers, 71, 89, 91, 92

concepts, in DOK framework, 31

conceptual understanding
- in DOK framework, 31
- and early numeracy skills, 57, 60
- and multiplication, 89
- problem-solving via, 77–78
- vs. rote memorization, 12, 114
- for teachers, 52–53

concrete manipulations, 15–16

confidence, 18, 26, 37

connection making, 12, 27, 30

conservation of numbers, 59

content creation, 10

counting, 58, 62–63, 70–71, 90

creativity
- celebrating variability and, 44
- in counting strategies, 63
- "do it like me" pedagogy vs., 22, 23
- in problem solving, 17

Culturally Responsive Teaching and the Brain (Hammond), 27

curriculum
- expectations as "hidden," 51
- high-quality materials in, 25
- meaningful/relevant, 27–30, 61, 77–79, 113
- start-time activities, 47–48

D

Daring Greatly (Brown), 111

decision making, 31

decomposition of numbers, 72, 89, 91, 92

Delpit, Lisa, 36

demographics, 11

Depth of Knowledge (DOK) framework, 30–32

dialogue
- among peers, 49
- in conceptual learning, 12
- math conversations, 13
- teacher-student, 50

difference, constant, 72–73

dignity distortions, 36, 37

disabilities, intellectual, 52

distributive property, 89, 90, 92

diversity
- and educational materials, 25–26, 38
- in STEM fields, 36
- in UDL framework, 12

division, 87–96, 98

"do it like me" pedagogy
- for fractions, 108
- historic approach to, 8–10
- redefining, 19–22, 114
- rote repetition in, 23
- and student identities, 11
- UDL framework vs., 12

Dolk, Maarten, 89

Dykema, Kevin, 26

Index

E
early numeracy skills, 55–66, 88
Echo, and rote repetition, 23, 24
EdReports, 25
education system
    high-quality materials in, 26
    system drivers in, 42
    systemic barriers in, 11–12
Edutopia, 3
EdWeek, 26
effect size, 40
emotional investment, 35
engagement
    belonging and, 45
    and math happiness, 113
    via meaningful tasks, 27, 33
    multiple means of, 13–15, 108
    in partner playlists, 35
    start-time activities for, 47–48
    and student interests, 47
enjoyment of math, 8, 18, 61, 112–114
equipartitioning, 99–100
equity
    via instructional improvements, 61
    in support services, 1–2
    and teacher/student identities, 10–11
    UDL to correct inequities, 11–19
Equity Trust, 24
equivalence, fractions and, 101–103
eudaimonic happiness, 113, 114
executive function, 18
expectations, high, 12, 38, 40
extended thinking, 31

F
fear of math, 88, 112
feedback, 75
first grade students, 69
Fitzpatrick, Billie, 4
fives frames, 62, 63, 65
Focus on Fractions: Bringing Research to the Classroom (Petit et al.), 109
Fosnot, Catherine Twomey, 89
fractions, 97–109
functions, teaching of, 16

G
games, 74
gifted and talented programs, 11
goals
    "firm goals, flexible means," 14, 89
    shared at start of class, 76
    student understanding of, 13–14
    of teachers, 5, 14
    of UDL, 18–19
Gordon, David, 4
group work, 33, 34
growth mindset, 35, 51, 75

H
Hammond, Zaretta, 27
happiness, of enjoying math, 112–114
Hattie, John, 40
hidden curriculum, 51
high-cognitive-demand tasks, 30–33
high school, 57, 97, 111
Howard, Dr. Tyrone, 45

I
identity
    differing teacher/student, 11
    math identity, 37, 52, 104, 107, 114
    and meaningful/relevant curriculum, 27
    and UDL inclusivity, 12
inclusiveness
    in assessment options, 18
    importance of, 2
    lesson example of, 20–22
    via presumed competence, 49
    and retraining for teachers, 10
    for student engagement, 47
    in support services, 1–2
    via three-legged learning stool, 40–41
    in UDL framework, 12, 19
individualized education programs (IEPs), 2, 11
inequities, 11–19, 37
interests, student, 30, 33, 47, 74, 80
interventionists, beliefs of, 44

isolated work, 20
iteration, fractional, 100–101

K
"keep, change, flip" rule, 10, 98
kindergarten students, 57, 69
knowledge, showcasing, 17–19

L
language barriers, 32
launch tasks, 48, 77
learning
    active vs. passive, 24
    celebrating mistakes in, 15
    co-created with students, 14–15
    dismantling barriers to, 113
    effect of teachers on, 40–45
    as growth/discomfort, 111
    nurturing environments for, 35–38, 107
    personalized, 16–17
    and presumed competence, 49–50
    purpose of, 14
    and student variability, 74
    trajectories, 89
    as "worthwhile," 15
lessons. *See* curriculum
lived experience, lessons relevant to, 27–30

M
marginalized students
    fostering belonging for, 26
    honoring humanity/identity of, 38
    math access for, 2, 11
    math statistics for, 3
    meeting the needs of, 25
    one-size-fits-all learning vs., 87
    teacher-student relationships for, 114
    tools for success for, 36
mastery, 3, 14
materials
    access to high-quality, 25–26
    criteria for, 25

mathematics
    anxiety about, 88
    college requirements for, 7–8
    everyday use of, 39–40, 57, 61, 63, 98, 107
    identity in relation to, 37, 52, 104, 107
    joy in, 8, 18, 61, 112–114
    proficiency statistics for, 2–3, 4
mathematics instruction
    accessibility of, 2–3
    as a civil right, 2, 4
    co-created with students, 12
    college-level, 8
    concept-based, 52–53
    critical improvements to, 61
    diverse opportunities in, 24
    engagement with, 13–15
    foundational skills in, 69
    historic competency cues in, 9–10
    identity considerations in, 38
    inclusive, 1–2, 114–115
    instructional materials for, 24–26
    procedural approach to, 8–10
    real-life scenarios in, 27
    via station rotation, 75
    and teacher assumptions, 43–45, 51–52
    teacher-centric, 9–10
    understanding lesson goals in, 13–14
"math people," 4, 5, 8, 44
meaningful/relevant tasks, 27–30, 61, 64–65, 77–79, 113
memorization, rote
    as a barrier, 88
    conceptual reasoning vs., 12, 60
    for fractions, 98
    historic approach via, 9, 11
    of multiplication tables, 87
    removing, 18
memory, working, 88
middle school, 97, 98, 103
mindset, student/teacher, 46, 50–51, 75, 107
mistakes
    celebrating, 15
    comfort with making, 19

Index

Moore, Shelley, 50
Moses, Robert, 2
motivation, student, 14, 45
multiplication, 16, 87–96
"Multiplication Is for White People": Raising Expectations for Other People's Children (Delpit), 36

N

National Council of Teachers of Mathematics (NCTM), 26, 61
National Teacher and Principal Survey (NTPS), 10, 11
Nation's Report Card, 2–3
No Child Left Behind Act, 7
number sense tasks, 48, 77
numeracy skills, 55–66, 88, 99
nurturing learning environments, 35–38

O

one-on-one student interviews, 17
oral processing, 16
ordering, fractions and, 103–104

P

partitioning, fractional, 100–101
partitive division, 94–95
part-to-whole concept, fractions and, 97
passive learning, 24
place values, 69, 71, 90
playlists, in blended learning, 34–35
preK students, 57, 69
problem-solving processes
    additive reasoning and, 68
    and conceptual instruction, 12–13
    foundations for, 77–80, 113
    and means of representation, 17
    multiple paths to, 69
    vs. rote memorization, 60
    station rotation for, 75–76, 83–84
    for subtraction, 80–84
procedural pedagogy, 8–10, 11
productive struggle, 60, 111–112
professional learning community (PLC), 36, 42

proficiency, demonstrating, 17–19
purpose, student, 18

Q

quantitative reasoning, 68
question asking, 13
quotative division, 94–95

R

racial issues, 10–11
real-life scenarios, 27, 33
reasoning
    additive reasoning, 57–58, 67–85, 90–91
    in DOK framework, 31
    fractional, 99–104
    in high-cognitive-demand tasks, 30
    multiple representations for, 16
    multiplicative, 88–89, 90
    quantitative, 68
    sense-making and, 3, 12, 61
recall and reproduction, 30
Rehabilitation Act 173, 1–2
relationships
    between multiplication and division, 94
    in nurturing learning environment, 35
    teacher cultivation of, 45–46
relevant curriculum, 27, 61, 77–79
repetition, rote, 9, 12, 51, 60
representation, multiple means of, 15–17, 32, 107
respectful environments, 35
rigorous education
    as a civil right, 4
    equitable access to, 2, 12
    expectations in, 12
    lack of access to, 2
    materials for, 25
    productive struggle in, 60, 111–112

S

second-grade students, 69, 71
self-assessments, 35
sense-making, 3, 9, 12, 33, 61, 78

sequencing
    forward and backward, 58
    fractions and, 103–104
skills
    building on additive, 69
    in DOK framework, 31
    numeracy skills, 55–66, 88
    teacher skill sets, 41–42
social-emotional factors, 15
spatial reasoning, 16
special educators, 43
station rotation, 75–77, 83–84
STEM fields, 7–8, 36
Stigler, Dr. James, 60
strategic thinking, 31
stress, 88
students
    academic tracking of, 9
    beliefs of, 44, 46
    choice for, 83, 89
    conceptual understanding of, 12–13
    early numeracy skills for, 55–66
    emotional investment by, 35
    empowering, 34–35, 113
    honoring humanity/identity of, 12, 18, 38
    as knowledge keepers, 17–19, 78, 88
    marginalized. *See* marginalized students
    as "math people," 4, 5, 8
    mindsets of, 46, 50–51
    Nation's Report Card statistics for, 2–3
    presumed competence of, 18, 26, 49–52
    racial identities of, 10–11, 36
    rote repetition by, 9–10, 23
    support services for, 1–2
    variability of, 12, 15
subitizing, 53, 58
subtraction, 29, 68, 69, 70–71, 72, 74–76, 80–84, 94, 103
success, student
    algebra as gatekeeper to, 3–4
    and in-class relationships, 46
    and early numeracy skills, 57
    and high-quality materials, 26
    and math happiness, 112
    and presumed competence, 49–50
    support for, 15
    and teacher expectations, 40, 49
    via three-legged learning stool, 40–44
    UDL as serving, 13
support services
    for high-cognitive-demand tasks, 32
    inclusive, 1–2
    options in, 14
    in purposeful learning, 74
support staff, 43
system drivers, 42

T

Tapper, Dr. John, 111
teachers
    articulation of goals by, 14
    beliefs of, 41, 42–45
    choices provided by, 14–15
    conceptual understanding of, 52–53
    expectations of, 40, 51
    goals of, 5
    materials available to, 25, 26
    math anxiety among, 112
    one-on-one instruction with, 75, 76
    procedures modeled by, 9–10
    racial identities of, 11
    relationship with students, 45–46
    retraining for, 10, 114
    in station rotation, 75, 76, 83
    and the three-legged learning stool, 40–45
    UDL framework considerations, 19
technology
    to demonstrate proficiency, 17–18
    representation via, 16
    in station rotation, 75, 83
tens frames, 15, 20, 62, 65, 70–71, 74, 75, 77, 103

Index

tests. *See* assessment
thought
    critical thinking, 60, 65, 78
    in DOK framework, 30–32
    encouraging deep, 24–25
    flexible, 69
    high-cognitive-demand tasks, 30, 32
    means for expressing, 17–19
    sharing/comparing student, 9, 12–13
timed work, 20, 74, 88
tracking, academic, 9, 11
Tucker, Catlin, 34

U

underserved students, 2, 3, 11, 114
unitizing, understanding of, 16, 89, 90, 91
Universal Design for Learning (UDL)
    action and expression in, 17–19
    additive reasoning with, 73–75
    to address inequities, 11–19
    barriers dismantled via, 113
    barriers to implementing, 42
    and early numeracy skills, 64–65
    engagement in, 13–15
    "firm goals, flexible means" in, 14, 89
    goal of, 12
    and high-cognitive-demand tasks, 32
    for math accessibility, 4, 40–41
    for multiplication/division, 89, 95, 107–108
    representation in, 15–17
    vs. rote memorization, 19–22
    station rotation activity, 75
usable materials, 25

V

values, number, 59–60
variability, learner
    additive reasoning and, 73–74
    and diverse representation, 15
    and early numeracy skills, 64
    and educational materials, 25–26
    and learning trajectories, 89–90
    organization and, 33
    and teacher assumptions, 51–52
    UDL for embracing, 12
Vermont Superintendents Association, 1
visual modeling, 10, 15–16, 17, 32, 74, 90, 103
voice, choice and, 12, 13, 46
vulnerability to examine assumptions, 111

W

Webb, Norman, 30
"Which One Doesn't Belong?" (WODB) activity, 48–49
whole-number reasoning, 99
word problems, 10
working memory, 88
"worthwhile" education, 15
written assessments, 17

Y

Young Mathematicians at Work: Constructing Multiplication and Division (Fosnot and Dolk), 89

About the Authors

Katie Novak, EdD, is an internationally renowned education consultant, author, graduate instructor at the University of Pennsylvania, and a former assistant superintendent of schools in Massachusetts. She has 20 years of experience in teaching and administration, a doctorate in curriculum and teaching, and 14 published books. Katie designs and presents workshops both nationally and internationally, focusing on the implementation of inclusive practices, Universal Design for Learning (UDL), multi-tiered systems of support, and universally designed leadership.

Ashley Marlow, MSEd, is an elementary math coach, a consultant, and the director of operations for All Learners Network (https://www.alllearnersnetwork.com/). She has 13 years of experience in teaching and coaching and is passionate about supporting teachers of experience in creating equitable learning opportunities in math. Ashley plans professional learning opportunities focusing on instructional routines in mathematics that support belonging, engagement, and access to rigorous grade-level content for all students.